ENCOUNTERS: *A Memoir*

Relationship Journeys from Around the World

D1648996

Sam Oglesby

SAM OGLESBY

Illustrations by Tobias Sugar

ISBN: 1-4392-6461-9
ISBN-13: 9781439264614
Library of Congress Control Number: 2009911574

⟦DEDICATION⟧

For Ari and the gang … you are always there for me.
And for my grandson, German Garcia.
The future belongs to you!

For my good swimming
phtna; Dawn!

May all your encounters
be happy ones!

Regards,

Sam

❧[CONTENTS]❧

PREFACE

Two things prompted me to write this memoir-ish collection of short stories: an old photo album and my birth certificate. When I "changed the front number" and turned seventy in August 2009, it really hit me that time was at a premium and that, to paraphrase a friend, I would probably be dust in ten years. If there were goals I still wanted to achieve, I had better not dally. The old Latin phrases *carpe diem, tempis fugit,* and *sic transit gloria* rang in my head.

A friend had drawn up a list of ten things she most wanted to do before she checked out. The list included things like meeting Michael Jordan and walking every block of

Manhattan. When I last checked with her, she had accomplished both of these feats and was well on her way to completing her wish list. Where was my list? I didn't have one other than the rather vague wish to be healthy, have a few good friends, and maybe ski once more before my knees collapsed. But being a competitive sort, I begin to think that maybe I should have a list too so I could tell my friend that I had ticked off ten fabulous happenings and was therefore as happy and fulfilled as she was! I decided that writing another book would be high on that list.

Several years ago, I had written my first book, *Postcards from the Past: Portraits of People and Places*. In that memoir, I described episodes from my life and the lives of other people—friends, family and even strangers—and now with the passage of time, I felt I still had experiences to share and issues to resolve. I had discovered in writing the first book the therapeutic value of putting words on a page. There had been things I wanted to ask and tell my parents before they died, and because of pride and youthful ignorance, I never had the chance to delve into some sensitive and painful areas of our lives that needed to have light shed on them.

I had confided to a friend that I felt deeply unhappy that I had not had the chance to apologize to my parents for some cruel, stupid things I did to them and thank them for bringing me into the world and making the many sacrifices they made to be able to give me the things they so generously provided me with. My friend suggested I write to my parents, and I did so via the stories in that first book. The effect was incredible, and I felt a dark cloud of guilt and self-recrimination lift, giving me relief that no shrink or medication could provide.

I realize that there are different strokes for different folks, but this was my way, or I should say my friend's way, which I adopted with great personal and emotional benefit. I am basically not an original person, although I am quite good at picking up on the suggestions and advice of others. I wish throughout my life that I had had more good advice from friends or even strangers. I am a great believer in the phrase successfully used by Hillary Clinton: "It takes a village." I often think of how many mistakes I could have avoided in my life if somebody had been there to guide me or even chide me. I am not planning to dish out advice in this volume, but maybe some of life's lessons I have learned will seep through the pages into the reader's consciousness.

That first book was rather easy to write. Aside from the stories related to me and my parents, describing the other people and places was a simple matter of pushing the memory button and letting the words flow. In those stories, I did not have to wrestle with difficult decisions about how much information to reveal and what details should be held back. I could write those accounts without worrying about hurting people or angering the subjects of my portraits. But there still remained stories to be told that would not flow so easily. I had left those tales out of my first endeavor and I found myself thinking, as time went by, that I really had to talk about what had been swept under the carpet. I hope what I write will emerge with a positive message.

Aside from my birth certificate reminding me how old I was, there was that dusty album containing pictures from the past. As often happens in life, you go looking for something and then find something else that is even more important. As I recall, several years ago I was looking for a picture of my father as a young man. Some of his Japanese friends were organizing a tribute to the work he had done in Japan and were assembling a story in photos of his life. I dug through the albums I had, and while doing so, came across another picture, a snapshot taken with one of those primitive Brownie cameras. It showed a little boy, a tow-headed white boy, standing at a wire fence, looking at three little black girls who were leaning into the wire, looking back at him. I stared at the photo for some minutes and then realized the little boy was me. I confirmed his identity when I flipped the picture over and saw in my mother's school marm handwriting: Sammy Oglesby, Girdletree, Maryland, Summer 1942. With the help of several older relatives, I reconstructed that meeting at the fence and wrote the following passage:

"African Americans were a sizeable part of our community on the Eastern Shore of Maryland, but I seldom saw them. Only once did I ever meet African American children my own age. It was by chance and for less than a minute, the time it takes to pluck ripe tomatoes from a few vines. During the high season, tomato-pickers swarmed the field near our farm. I used to watch them behind the wire fence bordering our property.

"One day, as I clung to the fence gazing at the rows of workers, three little black girls approached and grabbed the wire. For a few seconds, we swung together on the fence in a childishly improvised game, laughing as the fragile barrier sagged. One girl, a scholarly looking child wearing wire-rim glasses, tweaked my nose and said she wanted to marry me. Then she was gone as her parents moved to pick another row. From that brief, fence-swinging courtship, I never had the chance to speak to an African American socially until I went to high school twelve years later."

Time passed and I kept thinking about that long-ago encounter. Where were these little girls now? What had they done with their lives? What were they thinking when they saw me sixty-five years ago, peering at them through a wire fence? I thought of other passing encounters with people whom I would never know or speak to again. I recall once in Saigon, Vietnam, during the war, coming out of a building with a group of high-ranking American army officers. We were walking to waiting, chauffeur-driven vehicles that would take us to inspect some project that was designed to win hearts and minds and turn the war around in our favor. Everything was spit and polish: gleaming vehicles, highly polished shoes, crisp uniforms adorned with stars and eagles. As we proceeded, walking almost in lockstep, I looked to my right and saw behind barbed wire, only a few feet away, scores of emaciated Vietnamese laborers staring at us with empty eyes. My gaze locked with one of them who was staring at us. Who was he? What was he thinking? Did he hate us?

Then there was the time traveling overland from Arusha, Tanzania, to Nairobi, Kenya, when our Land Rover stopped for a few seconds so somebody could take a photo of the wildlife grazing on the distant savannah. As soon as our vehicle stopped, we were swarmed by tribespeople suddenly appearing from out of nowhere. They pressed their faces against the vehicle windows and looked at us as though we were curious creatures in a cage. Perhaps we were. I found myself thinking, what was their life expectancy? What made them happy? What made them sad? Human contact, however fleeting and seemingly impersonal, is a powerful experience.

Closer to home, I thought of the encounters, confrontations, liaisons, meetings, compacts, conflicts, affairs, and partnerships I had had in my life and wondered if writing about them would tell me anything that would guide me in those few years I had left before turning to dust, as my friend said we all surely would. One thing I knew for sure: I wanted only happy endings and no more bitter partings. I think two mistakes I made too often in the past were being my brother's (and sister's) keeper when I should have kept my distance from people even though I cared deeply about them, and not knowing that sometimes good fences make good neighbors. I have always been guilty of diving into relationships, and I now see from the vantage point of seven decades that rushing into intimacy can be a perilous journey. I'm not sure I can follow Lord Buddha's ideal of loving everybody equally, the homeless beggar in the street as much as your husband or wife or mother, but it is a good goal for which to strive.

I thought the photograph of the little girls and me would make a fitting cover for a memoir about encounters and relationships and what makes them so rewarding and challenging at the same time. I hope the three of them are happy wherever they are. They are probably older and wiser than I am!

Sam Oglesby

NEW YORK CITY
DECEMBER 2009

❧[CHAPTER ONE]❧

GIRDLETREE
Memories of Nowheresville and A Fragmented Childhood

I was born in 1939 and spent most of the forties on my grandmother's farm near a village called Girdletree on the eastern shore of Maryland. Calling Girdletree a village was probably bestowing more dignity on this benighted one-horse town than it deserved. My father, who grew up there, nicknamed it Whiffletree the Hick Town and said it had two of everything and a lot of nothing. By two of everything he was referring to the religious fissures that divided the place. Like bookends, there was a Baptist church at one end of town and a

Methodist temple on the other and two general stores in between. The Methodist store was Painey Pilchard's, and Mose Hudson owned the store to which Baptists went. Even in cases of dire emergency, like running out of toilet paper or sugar for baking, when Painey's was closed, a Methodist would never enter Mose Hudson's store. Years before, it was said, the two churches had reached a fever pitch of confrontation when a Baptist lady was allegedly insulted by a Methodist man.

The Baptists proceeded to raid the Methodist temple, dragging out its organ and dumping it in the river. The Methodists retaliated by stuffing burlap bags down the chimney of the Baptist church one Saturday night in December. When services were held the next morning and the church wood stove was lit, the sanctuary filled with smoke, driving the worshippers coughing and sputtering out onto the road, where most of the Methodist congregation was gathered with smirks on their faces. But to an outsider passing through on County Road 34 and those who were less informed about the politics of the village, Girdletree was just a nondescript collection of dwellings near a rural crossroads that disappeared into flat farmland bounded by the brackish-smelling Chesapeake Bay on one side and distant railroad tracks on the other. Aside from the noise of farm animals—chickens cackling and crowing at dawn, and cows groaning before mealtime—the only sounds we heard, day and night, were the pealing of church bells on Sunday morning and the train's shrill whistle during the night. It was a bucolic place.

Grandma and I lived alone together. Inside her house, whose exterior was shingled with asbestos, a faint smell of kerosene and kindling wood filled the air. Although my father had installed electricity in the house and had a full indoor bathroom built sometime in the thirties, my grand-mother never dreamed of using either of these modern con-veniences, considering these additions to be well-meaning but frivolous accoutrements. The closest we got to taking a bath was when my parents visited once and took a photo of me posing, but not bathing, in the tub. Washing our bodies be-yond the normal morning ablutions took place on Saturday night in the kitchen, when we had proper baths. A huge, circular zinc tub was dragged in from the pantry across the linoleum floor and filled with hot water that had been heated on the wood-fired cook stove in the kitchen. These weekly baths were rather painful. Grandmother scrubbed me with a wash rag till my skin was red, pointing to the grime and grit that turned the tub water gray, wondering how I had man-aged to get so dirty in just a week. She seemed to overlook the fact that a six-year-old who spent most of his time in the barnyard and the fields might pick up the odd speck of dirt. An outhouse in the backyard covered by riots of rose vines was our toilet, and a large, white enamel "slop jar" was carted upstairs every evening to serve nocturnal needs.

Except for the cozy, bright kitchen where we spent most of our time, the house was quiet and tomb dark. Hardly visible through half-gloom created by permanently drawn drapes, the living room was elaborately furnished with matching mohair chairs and a sofa of indeterminate color somewhere between gray and brown—the parlor "suit" my grandmother called them. A massive, claw-footed oak table with six high-back chairs inhabited the dining room from whose ceiling hung a chandelier that had never been illuminated. Neither room was ever used. In one corner of the dining room was a large Zenith combination radio receiver/record player covered by a gaudy Japanese silk fabric. My mother had brought it to the house along with her collection of Broadway musical recordings and Noel Coward plays, hoping to bring a bit of culture to what she regarded as a flat-world, hick wasteland. Quite the contrary effect was achieved. My grandmother resented this intrusion by a woman she had never liked. College-educated with a strong personality—and if that wasn't enough, her dark-skin and Catholicism were the final nails in her coffin—my mother didn't stand a chance with her mother-in-law, who could never have liked the woman who took away her beloved son and only child. So when my mother was not there, which was almost always, opening or even touching that electric contraption was forbidden. I never once heard it played.

Aside from the roar of a fire being lit in the kitchen cook stove or the pot-bellied wood-burner that gave us heat, the only sounds regularly heard in the house were the ticking of the clock on the dining room mantelpiece and the squeak of my grandmother's rocking chair, which she sat in after dinner while reading the Bible. Winding the clock every day was a serious evening ritual that I watched in awe, being told that one day when I had learned to do it, I might be allowed to wind the clock myself. The clock was a beautiful Seth Thomas made from early twentieth-century black plastic and embellished with clawed feet and little columns topped with gilded metal. Grandma related how she had saved up hundreds of Ivory Soap box tops over the years and, after mailing them into the clockmaker in Baltimore, had received the clock just after my father was born. That would have been 1911. My grandmother always referred to the clock in the feminine, saying, "She keeps good time."

My mother used to say in half-derisive whispers to my father that my grandmother—she called her by her given name, Nonie—kept the hours of a chicken, going to bed before nine o'clock and waking up at the crack of dawn or before. Ignorant of the country rhythms of early to bed, early to rise, my mother was the only person who ever dared turn on a switch to actually use the electric lights, which had been installed some years before. When Grandma and I were alone, which was nearly all the time, the only illumination after sundown was from kerosene lamps. It was surprising how much light two of these lamps could throw out through their tall, elegant glass chimneys; it was enough for me to do my homework when I reached school age and for Grandma to read her Bible, although what text she read she had certainly memorized years before. Our nightly ritual would end when we climbed the stairs to our bedrooms, slop jar in hand, and changed into nightshirts, which Grandma had stitched from empty sacks that had contained feed for pigs, chickens, and cows. Even after vigorous washing, the bags still retained the likeness of these animals stamped into the cloth, and a strange sight it was to see one of us gliding down the hallway, sporting the image of a pig on our nightshirt, lamp in hand, casting long, leaping shadows on the bare walls.

It was never clear to me why my parents deposited me with my grandmother for such long periods—years—of time. They seemed to be traveling and living in places connected to my father's work with chemical and biological warfare, which took him to research centers around the country. When he visited us and I touched the insignia on his uniform, he joked and called it the crossed douche bags, the symbol of the Army Chemical Corps. My parents often argued, and seeing them at odds with each other left me confused about who was right and wrong, which side I should support. I remember once my mother crying and then running out of the house into the fields behind the barn, my father saying nothing, just looking out into space at her as she disappeared into the rows of high corn, and my Grandmother, ever busy in the kitchen, just shaking her head.

To tell the truth, I was happier living with this clever peasant lady who had no formal schooling even though she had learned to read and write. Our life together was simple and punctuated by the needs of a small working farm. Even before I attended school, I was assigned chores and errands, feeding chickens, collecting eggs, and working in the vegetable garden that supplied most of our table needs. What we grew, we ate when it was in season, and the rest was canned, pickled, or, in the case of root vegetables, stored under the house for consumption during the winter. We slaughtered our own chickens, and neighbors brought fish and crabs from the bay as well as duck and deer meat from hunting expeditions. I think the formula for our contentment was the lack of idle time.

For my grandmother, there was the heavy but not unpleasant task of running a small, self-sufficient working farm. When she was not in the barn or working in the field, she was at her sewing machine or in front of the kitchen cook stove, which, fired with wood, baked the best bread and cooked the most delicious food I have eaten. Idle time was not spent drinking cocktails or listening to music, as my parents might do, but rocking and reading the Bible. There was also time for anecdotes, the favorite ones, often repeated, especially when my grandmother's sister, Aunt Mandy, and her brood descended on the house. Once, sometime in the thirties, coming back from Florida, they brought us a coconut, which my grandmother put in the front hallway, where it remained for the next forty years, a shriveled symbol of exotic items to be found in the world beyond Girdletree.

My grandmother was a native of Tangier Island, Virginia, an isolated spot in the middle of the Chesapeake Bay where the inhabitants had the strange custom of burying their dead in their front yards with little head stones so that each house had its own private cemetery. It had been settled in the early seventeenth century by English immigrants and remained a place apart ever since. No one came to the island or left it, and the natives' manner of speaking remains Shakespearean to this day.

While still a teenager, Grandma was widowed a few months after she married a Tangier waterman. He was drowned in a storm while crabbing in his sailboat on the bay. Some years later, she met her second husband, my paternal grandfather, a doctor, who had come to the island as its first physician. Never were there two people more different. He was a Virginia aristocrat, slender with delicate hands, who had a penchant for Bourbon and baseball. She was plain-spoken and stout, her speech laced with rustic turns of phrase: "Clean as a hound's tooth," "Pretty as wax" and other such homespun similes were part of her sentences whenever she spoke. She never addressed him by his first name during the entirety of their marriage, preferring to call him "Doctor." This strange second marriage lasted for the better part of two decades and produced a son, my father.

After a particularly severe winter when the bay was frozen for several months, preventing the arrival of provisioning ships from the mainland, my grandparents decided to move away from the island and ended up, for reasons unclear, in Girdletree, Maryland. After practicing country doctor medicine for nearly ten years and earning virtually no money—medical services to the farming community were usually exchanged for produce or other in-kind services—my grandfather died a pauper after several troubled years with a painfully broken hip that would not heal and which led him to self-medicating with increasingly heavy doses of morphine. In his final months, this kindly, intelligent man who had graduated first in his class at Johns Hopkins Medical School was reduced to a raving maniac when he couldn't find his needle for a pain-relieving injection.

His legacy was a twelve-year-old son and a widow with a small farm house and a few acres of land, but no money. Through hard work and thrift, they managed to survive and even send my father to college at the precocious age of sixteen. My grandmother recounted to me how he would mail his dirty laundry to her every week, and she would launder it and send it back to him at college. His mixture of shame and pride in his background—smart but poor and ignorant of the ways of the world—was described to me when he told me that he was the only gentile his Jewish classmates invited to join their study group and how he cried when his peers laughed at him for not knowing what a tuxedo was. He had received an invitation to a school dance, and on the card it was specified: Attire-Tuxedo. My father, as a freshman in college, had no idea what this was. After graduating with honors, he wanted to go to medical school and sought financial help from his father's wealthy Virginia family, the snobbish Oglesbys. Their response to this country bumpkin, whose mother of modest origins they had never approved of, was to send him a Bible. This gesture drove my father into a lifelong belief in populism and the common man.

For a variety of reasons mostly connected with the social ethos of rural America in the forties, my world was more circumscribed that it might normally have been. I was forbidden to cross the fields on either side of our house to visit the Jones family on the right or Niva Dukes and her daughters to the left. Furthermore, there were limitations on my traveling down the road towards the canning factory, where grandmother said trashy people lived. And under no condition was I to cross to the other side of the railroad tracks where the likes of Aunt Sadie, the colored lady, had her little house. I never got the full story from my grandmother about the Joneses, but apparently a feud had developed between my grandmother and Ada Jones, the family matriarch.

My grandmother felt that Miss Ada had snubbed her for no good reason. I once overheard my parents discussing this neighborly freeze and its possible causes, and they concluded that grandmother was considered somewhat "fast," having married once again, for a third time, not long after my grandfather, Dr. Oglesby, had died. In Girdletree society marriage was a one-time affair and widows were expected to stay that way till they went to their graves. In any case, Clayton Bowen, her third husband, turned out to be an unfortunate choice. Not long after the marriage, he suffered a massive stroke, which was followed by a bout of madness that resulted in his being carried away to the asylum in Cambridge, Maryland. For the longest time, I thought the word *Cambridge* meant "loony bin," having only heard the word used as in: "They took him away to Cambridge."

Niva Dukes was a different story. It was my grandmother who actually told me that Niva was a "fast" woman. I would see her in the post office on Main Street from time to time. She would smile and pat me on the head and sometimes give me a dime. She was an attractive, Belle Watling figure, generously made up and always turned out in expensive clothes. My grandmother would hiss to me when Niva was out of earshot, "Wonder where she got those clothes on a factory worker's salary." Even to my juvenile mind, the answer to that question could be found in the shiny, late-model cars that often pulled up into Niva's driveway of an evening. Aunt Sadie was a different story. There was no moral or social smear attached to this grandmotherly figure. It was a matter of race.

When I asked my grandmother why I could not visit Aunt Sadie's, her reply had a brevity that breached no discussion or questioning. "She's colored; she's a Negro. Aunt Sadie's a good woman, but she's not our kind." The forbidden being so tempting, I violated her no-go rule more than once, climbing the hill that rose sharply from the road to Aunt Sadie's modest, unpainted clapboard house, the kind of dwelling that today would appear quite chic in one of those over-exposed Abercrombie & Fitch ads featuring boney models striking moody poses in front of an abandoned shack in a South Hampton-ish setting.

Aunt Sadie was always baking, and her kitchen was redolent with the perfume of pies and cakes and vanilla extract, which she used not only to flavor her pastries but also as a kind of perfume that she applied directly to her skin. When I asked her why her skin smelled so sweet, she laughed and threw up her hands, saying, "Why, chile, that's cause I put vanilla on me!" She would demonstrate her secret by taking a small, dark little bottle out of her apron pocket, putting dabs on what she called her pulse points, behind her ears, and on her wrists. When I said I wanted to try some, too, her ample body shook as she giggled and anointed me with her vanilla extract formula. "Now you shoo on home, Sammy Oglesby. You smell like a fried pie or some kinda French floozie, I dunno which!"

Apparently the smell lingered longer than it should have. When I got home and entered the kitchen, Grandma squinted at me with suspicion and screwed up her nose. "You've been to Aunt Sadie's again, haven't you? And I'm gonna tan your hide. That'll teach you a lesson." It was not the first or the last thrashing I got from my grandmother. There was no "spare the rod" in her household.

Until I started first grade at the two-room school house a mile up the road, I almost never encountered a child my own age, let alone had a friend who was a contemporary. The closest thing I had to a friend was the ill-tempered Miz Idlelette, a cranky old woman almost as wide as she was tall, which was well under five feet. Miz Idlelette lived alone in the tiniest of houses down the road on the way to town, that pathetic collection of general stores, a barbershop, the post office, and the Worcester County Farmers' Exchange, a defunct bank that had gone bust in 1929. Peering through its barred windows, one could imagine the chaos that had reigned on that day almost twenty years earlier when the bank shut down. Account books and deposit slips were still scattered everywhere, and a bank teller's green celluloid visor lay on the dusty floor. At Miz Idlelette's, I was always offered something to eat, mostly items of uncertain provenance and freshness. That was before "use by ..." came into fashion, and I remember more than once Miz Idlelette surreptitiously scraping greenish mold from a curling piece of bread before offering it to me. Almost no conversation passed between us, and I spent most of my visits there watching Miz Idlelette smoke cigarettes.

I had never seen a woman smoke before, and Miz Idlelette had a particularly fascinating way of dealing with her vice. Somehow she managed to double inhale so that smoke ingested into her mouth would be blown out shortly after the puff and reinhaled into her nostrils, creating a dragonish effect that absolutely fascinated me. I could sit for hours on end watching her double inhale smoke and she accommodated me by usually chain-smoking one Camel after another. As a result of her incessant dragon habit, her upper lip was a dark brownish color, giving her a little Hitler moustache. When Miz Idelette was not smoking, I could entertain myself by looking at the many plates from various places that adorned her kitchen walls. There was one from a Chicago World's Fair and another one with a painted picture of a factory on it that said "What Trenton Makes, the World Takes." Although I was not, strictly speaking, forbidden from visiting her, my grandmother expressed her disapproval of Miz Idlelette with a frown and the dismissive two words, "She smokes."

Miz Idlelette did have one story she used to tell me from time to time and that was about how she had vomited up her tonsils when she was a little girl. When I visited her, I constantly nagged Miz Idlelette to repeat her gruesome tonsil tale. It was only when she was in the best of moods that she would accommodate me with this disgusting, wonderful account. When I asked why she had regurgitated her tonsils instead of going to the hospital to have them removed as I did, she replied, "Cuz they was rotten! End of story! You had enough, Sammy Oglesby? You are one strange chile, if I do say so!"

From time to time, usually once or twice a year, my grandmother's sister, Aunt Mandy, and her daughters, Cousin Inez and Cousin Lillian, would arrive in Inez's maroon Plymouth for an overnight visit. The highlight of these trips would occur in the afternoon when the ladies would sit on the front porch in rockers and drink iced tea. The topics of conversation covered during these porch hangouts would focus mostly on births, deaths, and other *sic transit gloria* events, interspersed occasionally by Cousin Inez relating what passed for off-color stories. Her favorite joke, which she often repeated with no apparent detriment to the volume of laughter that acknowledged it, involved a man getting on a trolley car. He had a suitcase in one hand and a shopping bag in the other. Trying to be helpful, the lady passenger next to him asked, "Sir, can I put your token in for you?" He replied, "Oh, I didn't know it was hanging out!" The wails and shrieks that accompanied this punch line were ear-splitting.

Cousin Lillian, known to us as Cousin Peaches, was more retiring and must have been beautiful when she was young. She had moved from the country in the thirties and got a government job in Washington DC, where Cousin Inez also lived with her husband, Sam Butler. Cousin Inez was a true eccentric. She bought a new wedding ring with a larger stone and a new Plymouth every year on the rents she got from letting out rooms to Korean exchange students. She lived in the Mount Pleasant section of Washington DC, in a crumbling Victorian town house that my father had nicknamed Ptomaine Towers due to its unkempt and actually rather dirty condition and because my mother claimed to have gotten food poisoning there from something Cousin Inez had served her. Once she invited me to Washington for a visit. Her house was straight out of a Charles Addams cartoon. Green velvet portieres covered the windows, creating an interior gloom, making it hard to see where one was going. Two nasty terriers would dart out from under the dining room table and bite my ankles. The only thing we did outside of her house was to go to a double-feature film, which she insisted on sitting through twice, subjecting me to nearly eight hours of Charlton Heston parting the Dead Sea. Cousin Inez decided on impulse that I needed to have my hair bleached, so she took a bottle of peroxide to my head, and I returned to Girdletree looking like an albino, much to the horror of my grandmother and the derision of my classmates, who had already decided I was a square peg in a round hole.

Sweet and cheerful, Cousin Peaches always seemed a bit dazed to me. Although unmarried, she referred to a man named Harry as her husband. When I asked my grandmother about Harry and where he was, she explained that one time riding on a train between Washington DC and Baltimore, Cousin Peaches had met a young soldier on his way to France to fight in the First World War. They shared a seat on the train and had exchanged names and addresses, and later he wrote her letters from Ypres or one of those foreign-sounding places when he was fighting on the Western front. After a time, the letters stopped coming and one could only speculate that Harry had been killed. My father cruelly suggested that Harry had probably met some cute French mademoiselle and had just forgotten Cousin Peaches, but Cousin Peaches always told people that she lost her husband in the First World War.

Without knowing it, Cousin Peaches was somewhat of a Civil Rights pioneer. Shortly after she moved to Washington DC, southeast Washington to be exact, her neighborhood became black almost overnight. The creation of jobs during the Depression had drawn flocks of African Americans from the fields of the Dixie Belt to the nation's capital, and most of them settled in Cousin Peaches' neighborhood, creating a white flight to the Maryland and Virginia suburbs. Cousin

Peaches, a shy Southern woman, was rather proud to be the last white holdout on her block and told us that her black neighbors were far nicer than the whites they had replaced. Asking the rhetorical question, "Why should I run away from my house? I own it, don't I?" Cousin Peaches stayed put and never regretted it for a minute. Her firm stand left a strong impression on me, which was to resonate years later when I was a student at the lily-white University of Virginia.

My first five years had been spent mostly in the company of old women—my grandmother and on occasion her sisters and their already aging daughters and the Camel-inhaling Miz Idlelette—so my social skills with other types of people, especially children of my own age group, were virtually non-existent. I remember the first day of school in the fall of 1945 when I entered Miss Grace Dickerson's class. Miss Dickerson was a maiden lady school marm who had been my father's first grade teacher twenty-eight years earlier. She presided over one room, in the center of which was a pot-bellied wood stove. The classroom was divided, in what seemed to be no particular order, to accommodate the three grades that were housed in that one room. So Miss Grace taught the three grades more or less at the same time. There were no problems because discipline was strict. Across the hall in the other room was the principal, Mrs. Watson, who also served as the teacher for grades four to six. It was common knowledge that Mrs. Watson had a long ruler that she used without hesitation when either her students or Miss Dickerson's needed to be brought in line.

My first day of school was not auspicious. My grandmother had decided to dress me in a sailor suit, which was in fashion for little boys during those war years. One of my front teeth was missing, as was a large swath of hair on my forehead. I had sent a lock of my hair and a photo to my father, who by then was fighting in the Pacific. When I entered the classroom, I got stares and silence. All of the other boys were dressed in dungarees. Somebody shouted, "What's wrong with your hair?" Another child, a squeaky little girl, asked me why I was wearing that funny suit. Later, we were each asked to introduce ourselves to the class and tell everybody what we liked best. When my turn came, I told my peers that I liked picking red roses by the outhouse and smelling them. A derisive roar emanated from the class and somebody shouted, "Pretty flowers!" From that moment on in school, I was known as Pretty Flowers. The name stuck. I remember coming back to Girdletree more than twenty years later as a Vietnam veteran and running into one of my old classmates in the barbershop. He looked at me for a moment, blinked, and then, with a flash of recognition, grinned and said, "Well, whaddya know! It's Pretty Flowers!"

Rejected by my classmates and limited in other ways from wider social contacts, I turned inward, relying increasingly on my own fantasies and imagination. At some point, I discovered the attic in my grandmother's house. I would spend as much time as I could in this retreat without arousing my grandmother's questions and reproaches. "What are you doing up there? A boy's got no business foolin' around in an attic! Get down here where you belong!" The attic was a wondrous place. The wind whistled and moaned in the rafters. There was an indescribable odor up there, a scent of the past, musty but not unpleasant; everything smelled old. There were stacks of old books and steamer trunks full of antique clothes. Flappers' dresses, wedding clothes from a bygone era, a cutaway with tails, and a jar full of peacock feathers. I tried on all of the clothes, singing and giving speeches to nobody in particular, staring out the tiny attic window at the long rows of tomato plants being worked in the field beyond our land by black workers trucked in from the South.

Another discovery I made was in the never-used front parlor. There was a wind-up Victrola partly hidden behind the mohair sofa. It contained stacks of records, mostly World War I ballads and Hawaiian-themed songs. I learned how to crank up His Master's Voice, and before long I had learned the words to "There's Long, Long Trail A-Winding," "Hullo Hawoyah, How Are Ya?" and "Ukelele Lady," among others.

It was at this point in my young life that I fell in love with the past and came to realize that I had no one to rely on but myself, that friends only existed in the fantasy attic of my mind. I saw myself as a fly on the wall, watching others but never participating. What seemed happy and beautiful to me were things that had already happened, things that I never participated in myself but merely watched or heard about or created in my increasingly fantasy-prone mind.

In 1948, I moved to Japan with my parents. We came back to the States and visited Girdletree once or twice before I returned to America for college in 1956. During school holidays, I usually came to Girdletree in the winter, or for summer vacations we went to Ocean City, Maryland, where my grandmother worked as a companion caretaker to an elderly lady, a woman who was actually about my grandmother's age. She remained the most important figure in my life, a reference point of stability and positive energy that I never again found in any other living being. I limped through college in what must have been one of the most mediocre six-year careers that ever earned a BA degree. My grandmother congratulated me and said diplomatically that she would hang my diploma on the highest hook in the house, which she did when I got it in August 1962.

After graduation, I went back to Girdletree late that summer with no particular plan in mind. I seemed to have no ambition and was content to just drift and sit on the back porch looking out into space. One evening in October, as I stood outside in the yard watching my breath vaporize and listening to the crunch of frozen grass as I stomped my feet, my grandmother appeared at the kitchen door, and with a note of urgency in her voice, told me that the president was going to address the nation. I listened to Kennedy say that there was a Cuban missile crisis. A couple of days later, I got a "Greetings" letter from the draft board inviting me to join the U.S. army. Shortly thereafter, I left Girdletree for boot camp and what Grandma described as my globetrotter's life.

Over the next five years, I moved from Libya, which was then a kingdom, to Switzerland and then to Vietnam, where the war was escalating to a bloated disaster. Throughout my time abroad, my grandmother and I corresponded regularly, and I promised her I would return in the early spring of 1968 when I finished my tour of duty in Vietnam. She said, half joking, in a letter to me that I had better hurry up because she was getting old. I never felt age or illness had anything to do with my grandmother. She was such a tower of strength that I thought she would live forever; the prospect of her dying one day, even though she was already in her eighties, just did not seem possible.

I flew back to the States in April 1968, landing in Washington DC the day that Martin Luther King was shot. The city was in flames, and I was confused and depressed. I had just come from a stupid war where people were killing each other for no reason, and now I had returned to my home country to find the same thing happening. I took the bus from DC to Baltimore and then to Salisbury, Maryland, where I was picked up by grandma's neighbor. When I got off the bus and saw his face, I knew what had happened. Will Ingersoll shook my hand with sadness and simply said, "Samuel, you got here too late. She died last night."

We drove to the farm without speaking, and I thanked him when he let me out in the backyard near the barn.

The back door was unlocked, and I entered the kitchen to find half-eaten food on the table and a cooked meal on the wood stove. I lifted the lid of one of the pots and smelled black duck stew, my favorite dish. I later learned from Miz Conway, her neighbor, that Grandma had prepared it for me as my welcome home dinner. I walked through the house like a visitor in a museum and found myself in the gloomy old dining room where bits of dust danced in the narrow shaft of light that peeped in through the curtains. As I walked past the dining room table, I bumped into the old Zenith record player that had almost never been used. Suddenly, strangely, almost miraculously, it started to play. It was Betty Garrett singing from the Broadway musical *On the Town*. Her voice reached out over the scratchy recording with the haunting words "There's so much more embracing still to be done, but time is racing!" I didn't bother to lift the record player's lid but just moved on to the living room and then to the front porch, where the old ladies used to sit, as her voice faded away with "Oh well, we'll catch up some other time!"

[CHAPTER TWO]

SO WHAT IF IT TOOK ME SIX YEARS TO GET A BA?

It was Christmas Eve, 1958, sleeting wet snow, and I had just been fired from my job. It was a small job; I was a junior clerk at a bank in Philadelphia. I was nineteen years old and I had just flunked out of the University of Pennsylvania. Now I was jobless and homeless, having been thrown out of the apartment I shared with a friend who was tired of my not paying my share of the rent and eating the food in the fridge that he had bought. How did I come to this sad state? I had been raised in an environment of privilege and placed in an Ivy League school when I was seventeen. What had gone wrong? Why was I on the streets?

I was the classic example of the best laid plans gone awry. Raised by caring parents who were products of the Great Depression and who had fought their way out of poverty, vowing to give their children everything they had been deprived of, I was a model, straight-A student until I was fifteen. Then something happened to my mind and my attitude, and I suddenly became, to paraphrase my father, no longer serious. Doing homework was silly and uncool; in fact, everything seemed stupid. Without realizing it, I had become a teenage nihilist. Hanging out, smoking, and riding in our 1950 Ford were the only things I was interested in doing. I stopped talking to my parents. "Where did you go?" "Out." "What have you been doing?" "Nothing." Beyond that terse exchange, we never spoke.

Somehow I managed to finish high school, even skipping the eleventh grade. My rationale for this accelerated academic journey was that school was so boring and worthless, I'd better get it over with as quickly as I could. This stage of my lackluster life coincided with the appearance of the film *Rebel Without a Cause*, which reinforced my feeling that doing nothing and being disgusted with life was the right way to live. This film signaled the advent of the anti-hero in American youth culture, and I was greatly influenced by the negative, glamorous role model of James Dean. Later when he died in a car crash at age twenty-four, our high school went into mourning and most of the students wore black arm bands.

Expecting a series of rejections from colleges, my parents were beside themselves with delight when I got into the University of Pennsylvania. My father insisted that I enroll in the Wharton School of Finance and Commerce, saying, "He who controls the money, controls everything." I had no interest in any kind of control at that point in my life and, truth be told, had no interest in anything. I was the classic case of a young person who needed to have a gap year, as the Brits often do, or join the army or sign up as an oiler on a tramp steamer. But being upper middle-class, these unorthodox approaches were not an option.

I should have had the luck of my neighbor, Ed Katlas, who graduated from high school with me. His father gave him a thousand dollars and said, "Son, there's the door. Go out into the world and do something." And Ed did. He joined the California forestry department and had a splendid life. I learned about all of this at a high school reunion fifty years later, and I wished I had followed his example. But hindsight is 20/20, and I had no independence of mind when I was sixteen. In retrospect, looking back through the prism of many decades, it is easy to see that I had been placed in the worst possible situation. Had my parents thrown me out of the house and told to get on with my life, I'm sure I would have landed on my feet and done something. As it was, the umbilical cord in the form of unlimited money and unwanted advice was given to me, which resulted in my developing a sulking, resentful dependence on good-hearted people who only wanted the best for me. But since my father had practically posed for my college application photograph, there was no turning back and, booted and suited in a forties-style double-breasted outfit that was to garner hoots and jeers when I got to Penn's hollowed ivy walls, I boarded a propeller-driven DC-6 for the long journey across the Pacific from Japan to the United States.

In those days of more leisurely, pre-jet travel, the plane journey involved island-hopping, and I remember spending the night on Wake Island and later in Hawaii. Since I was traveling on MATS (Military Air Transport System) because my father worked for the U.S. Defense Department, I was billeted in military barracks in these stopovers and recall sharing a room with a young marine lieutenant at Hickam Air Force Base in Honolulu. He told me how lucky I was to have everything handed to me on a silver platter. He said he had grown up as a share-cropper's son in the rural south and had had to fight for everything.

He had joined the marines and worked his way up through the ranks, becoming an officer by the time he was twenty-five. Working my way up the ranks or working at anything was totally alien to what I had known in my pampered life, which included servants at home and being deferred to by almost everybody because of my father's position. We went around Honolulu together and visited the only two hotels in town at that time, the Royal Hawaiian and the Moana. In the Royal Hawaiian, there was a drinking fountain, but instead of water, it had pineapple juice flowing from the spout.

I found my way back to the East Coast and spent a few days with my grandmother on her farm in Girdletree, Maryland, before heading for Washington DC and then Philadelphia. My reappearance in Girdletree was instructive to me insofar as the sociology of village life and what causes a person to be accepted or viewed as an outsider by a homogenous group of rural, working-class people. I had lived part of my childhood in Girdletree and always felt myself one of them, but my now being a college student placed me in a separate, foreign category.

Contemporaries who had been my schoolmates several years earlier no longer called me Sammy; they now addressed me as Samuel, and the easy banter that had been part of our rapport no longer existed. I was a stranger. Girdletree, to my knowledge, had never fathered a college graduate. Its male citizens were all farmers, fishermen, or laborers of one sort or another. To be sure, there was the village barber, and the two preachers who ministered in the rival village churches had had higher education, and the two-room school house had school marms who had been trained at normal schools. But among ordinary citizens, there were no college graduates and almost no high school grads, either. Typically, education stopped at the sixth grade or, at most, at the end of junior high school.

With sadness, I realized I was an outsider, a fate that would seem to dog me throughout my life. And so it was with mixed feelings that I said good-bye to Girdletree and its denizens, knowing I would never be a part of that community as I had once fantasized I would. One day I had arrived there from overseas thinking I had come home. Two days later, I left realizing I was a stranger. Who was it who said "You can never go home again?" This experience was one of many in my life where I saw the results of my opposing roots—working class and upper class—producing confusion and conflict, sometimes putting me in awkward situations in supposedly classless America.

I stopped in Washington DC to meet up with a high school classmate who was also going to Penn. He was heading for the school of architecture and had been voted school clown our last year of high school even though I knew he was an unhappy person at heart. The night before we left for Penn, we went out in his father's station wagon looking for an open road where we could get the car up to a hundred miles an hour. With Elvis blaring on the car radio and the wind roaring in through the open windows, we hit the hundred mile mark and then decided it would be cool to play chicken with other cars on the highway.

After a few half-hearted attempts to challenge the oncoming headlights, we came to our senses and headed home. Somehow, we survived the evening having gotten our kicks without killing ourselves. Many years later, I read in *Connoisseur Magazine* that my friend had died of AIDS. The article said he had kept his sense of humor to the very end of his life. Commenting on his rapid loss of eyesight due to the disease, he confided to his friend, the Countess of Poulignac, that at that point "seeing for me {was} like looking through olive oil."

Billy McCarty had become very rich as an interior designer to the jet set and lived in London, where he had a world-class art collection valued at hundreds of millions of dollars. He also had a chateau in France, where he gave grand dinner parties and was very particular about hanging game for just the right amount of time before it was cooked. Who would have guessed that our rather pathetic high school clown would end up leading such a glamorous life? And he never even managed to get his architecture degree. But he was always a good networker and could make people laugh.

I hated Penn from the first day I got there. My two suite mates in the dorm, Warwick House, were obnoxious preppies who were two years older than me. The first thing they said to me was that Warwick was pronounced without sounding the second W, as in Warick. "You didn't know that, did you?" they smirked. One had gone to Groton and conspicuously added the Roman numeral three after his name, so we called him Three Sticks. Even in the dead of winter, he kept the windows open, saying we needed fresh air and that in boarding school they had told him that cold air was healthy.

I had just turned seventeen, and at that age, two years difference in age is an immense gap. Instead of being mentored, I was ridiculed. They were sophisticated and made fun of me when I knelt by my bed and said prayers every night. They laughed at my strange clothes and put me down every time they had the chance, even teasing me about wearing braces on my teeth. The academic side of Penn was no better. Added to the fact that I had no interest in accounting and statistics, the professors were boring teaching assistants doing time teaching freshman classes as part of their graduate program requirements; they did nothing to stimulate my imagination and desire to learn.

In every subject except English, I had failing or near failing grades. It was strange that a so-called world-class university had no counseling or advisory service to guide seventeen-year-olds through the daunting social and academic maze that the first year in university presents. I was totally on my own, and joining a fraternity turned out to be a disaster. I was introduced by my English professor to the fraternity I ended up joining. He was a nice enough person, but the brothers in the fraternity were for the most part a self-destructive bunch indulged in stupid capers, like flying a Nazi banner from the flag pole of the fraternity house. During my second semester, I simply stopped going to classes. I spent a month staying up all night and sleeping all day, reading all of the books and plays of Tennessee Williams and Truman Capote and smoking tons of Winston cigarettes. Sun-deprived, I developed a pasty, white complexion not unlike a decadent geisha. I subsisted on White Castle hamburgers and coffee.

I flunked-out after two semesters and ended up in Washington, DC staying with my uncle, my mother's younger brother. When their mother-my grandmother-died, my uncle was only twelve or thirteen years old and my mother took him into our family and raised him as her own son forcing him to study and graduate from high school. It was obvious that he and his wife had no time for me and only tolerated my presence as a grudging payback for my mother having raised him. This was perhaps the lowest point in my young life. I was confused, rejected by my university, friendless, utterly lacking in a sense of direction and staying with people who didn't like me.

At this point, my survival instinct began to surface and I managed, through family connections, to get accepted via the backdoor into the University of Virginia. My sponsor was a relative on my paternal grandfather's side of the family who was chairman of the mathematics department at the university. He was well-known in his profession and had devised an approach to that science that was referred to colloquially as "whorehouse mathematics." I never found out what that label meant even as I struggled through the university's basic math requirement during summer school.

In the early sixties, living in Charlottesville, Virginia, and going to "the university" was a surreal experience for somebody who had been raised in Japan in an international environment where racial origin was not an important consideration. I had attended a high school where the president of the student body had been black and where dozens of ethnic identities had been represented, from white Russian refugees to Hawaiians, Filipinos, Koreans, and Germans. In those days of legal segregation in Virginia, the university was lily-white and the town was also governed by whites-only regulations that forbid mixing of the races.

Sitting at lunch counters in local diners was forbidden to blacks, and the races were segregated in movie theaters, with balconies designated for African Americans and the downstairs orchestra sections reserved for whites. Listening to their divergent reactions to the punch lines in films, I came to realize that black and white audiences had distinctly different senses of humor.

Weekend football games were the highlight of the fall season. To me, they were strange events, with black spectators limited to seating in the end zones of the football field. From a vantage point of fifty years later, it seems incredible to me that such a society could have even existed, let alone present a veneer of happy contentment with seeming friendliness between the races and cheerful acceptance of second-class status by those who were discriminated against. I knew it was a charade when I met the only African American I would know socially during those years. She was a student at a black college outside of town and the girlfriend of a white classmate. They met clandestinely in his apartment in the evening.

One night I was invited to his place for dinner. She had promised to cook smothered chicken for us, a dish that my friend had raved about, something only found in homes and not in restaurants. I arrived at his place on time and was surprised to see that his windows were dark. Had I come on the wrong evening? I climbed the stairs to his floor, and when I knocked, the door was opened immediately by my friend. "Come in quickly!" he said with urgency.

I entered and noticed the black curtains drawn over his windows, and he explained, "We have to do it this way. Otherwise there would be trouble for Deenie." We had our dinner and enjoyed each other's company. But when I took my leave and they bid me good night, I saw fear and sadness in their eyes.

For those of us with the right social connections and the correct skin pigmentation, or lack thereof, life at the University of Virginia was sweet. There was the Farmington Country Club for weekend relaxation and golf, and polo games at Brook Hill Farm, my uncle's estate on the outskirts of town. Fraternity parties were a weekly event, with young lovelies imported from the women's colleges down the road. Classes were reasonably interesting and not too demanding, and from time to time there would be appearances by well-known people like William Faulkner, who came to the university one spring to deliver a series of lectures. Another famous visitor was Ralph Bunche, the African American assistant secretary general from the United Nations who came to give a talk on his work in the world of diplomacy and international relations.

The touchy matter of Virginia's segregation laws and how they would affect Dr. Bunche were side-stepped when he was offered overnight accommodation in the president's house and entertained on campus, saving this world-renowned figure the humiliation of being refused service in one of the local greasy spoons.

In my senior year, I met a lovely girl. She was sweet and intelligent, and I could see through the layers of baby fat she still carried with her that she would soon be a beauty. After we began seriously dating, she limited herself to eating carrots and celery, and my prediction was fulfilled; she was stunning and gorgeous. We spent lazy summer days together taking a bottle of wine and a blanket to the fields on her father's farm, where we laughed and loved under the blue sky.

Although no words were spoken, it was understood that we would probably marry. She came from a super-rich background. Her family was one of the Fortune 500, and I realized tying the knot with her would mean that I would never have to lift a finger again or worry about finding a job. Was this what I wanted? I was not sure. Her parents were uninspiring coupon-clippers, and I could see the dead end side of such a gilded life. I was also not sure of my own feelings. My attraction to men had become obvious to me. Did I want to lead a double life and probably end up a two-timing alcoholic?

As I traveled back to Girdletree to give my grandmother the college diploma she had waited so long to see and to meet her for what would be the last time, I had a lot on my mind. But these weighty life decisions would have to be put on hold. In the meantime, my attention was diverted by a short letter I had received from the draft board. The morning mail had brought Greetings! telling me that I had been conscripted into the U.S. army and that I was to report to Fort Jackson, South Carolina, within thirty days. I had managed to stumble through university in spite of myself and get a degree. Not a very good degree, but it was a piece of paper. Now I had to think about what I would do in this next chapter of my life.

CHAPTER THREE

WHEN KHADDAFI WAS A LIEUTENANT
My Life as a Grunt in the Kingdom of Libya and Other
Glamorous Locations

Not long ago, I came across a diary entry I had written a few years back. It went like this:

"Two weeks after graduating from college in the summer of 1962, I received a letter in the mail that began with a terse 'Greetings!' I had been drafted into the U.S. army."

Among my upper-middle-class circle of white friends at the University of Virginia, I was the only one to be honored with this invitation. Everybody else had had the presence of mind to enroll in grad school, find a "critical" job, or otherwise orchestrate their way out of conscription. Before you could say "Fort Benning, Georgia," I found myself with a shaved head, swallowed up in baggy khaki fatigues, and riding a bumpy train to Columbia, South Carolina, with a motley collection of other young recruits. Not a college grad in the carload except for me.

My real education and debut into the world was about to begin. Raised in an atmosphere of ease and privilege—we had full-time servants at home and one of them used to even tie my sister's shoes for her—I had never seen a black person in a non-servile position, except for Dr. Ralph Bunche, who had made a rarified speaking appearance at the University of Virginia when I was an undergraduate there. To me, African Americans were what you might call "background" people. Always there but never the center of attention, always helping but never getting credit for anything and often being scolded for minor, fancied infractions. "Jerome, I told you to water those geraniums real good, and now look at 'em! The sun has dried 'em to a frazzle and it's all your fault."

Imagine my surprise when our boot camp train was met by a six-foot-four-inch black master sergeant who glared at our rag tag group of mostly white boys and roared, "Stand up on your hind legs and salute me, you miserable worms!" As the grueling routine of boot camp unfolded, we were too numb and exhausted to remember who we had been and were still confused about what we were becoming. Then changes occurred. We became strong, and our uniforms fit us. A camaraderie, unimaginable a few weeks earlier, began to grow. That Jewish guy from New York and the Chicano from Texas became my friends.

One midnight, in a dark pine forest as cold rain pounded my face and my rifle seemed to weigh a thousand pounds on the last mile of a forced march, the big black guy from Detroit relieved me of my unbearable load. Strangest of all, we started to love and respect the dreaded master sergeant. My earlier life as a Virginia gentleman seemed faraway, unreal and irrelevant. During those months, we learned many things, from first aid to firing a machine gun, but most important, when we graduated from basic training, we had become men who possessed compassion and understanding for our fellow beings, real compassion untainted by racial discrimination or economic distinction.

The army changed my life and gave me focus and direction that I might never have gained otherwise—the same for my GI buddies from inner cities, Tex-Mex border towns, and snake-worshipping hollows in Appalachia. Though different as night and day, we had in common our youth. We were still malleable enough to learn life's lessons before the miasmic veil of prejudice and ego had put scales on our eyes. We were part of that great social incubator, the U.S. military, that started the domestic racial revolution in 1948 when, by executive order of President Truman, it integrated blacks and whites into its ranks. I might never have learned to live meaningfully and equally with my fellow Americans had I not been drafted that sleepy summer of 1962.

As much as I cherish my military service and the lessons it taught me, I have mixed feelings about reviving the draft today. The army and other branches of the military are first-class finishing schools for turning boys and girls into responsible men and women and will continue to take youngsters off under-privileged streets and pampered campuses and turn them into solid, right-thinking citizens. But leave this to an all-volunteer army. Turning back the clock by reinstituting compulsory military service cannot work in today's radically changed America. It would probably result in widespread resistance, adding to the social problems already plaguing our cities. We have already seen how time ran out on the draft when it was used in Vietnam, triggering urban riots, numerous desertions, insubordination in the ranks, a GI drug problem of epidemic proportions, "fragging" of officers on the front lines, and massive protests on campuses like Kent State, where unarmed students were killed by National Guard rifles.

Not only would it be difficult to bring back the draft for social reasons, it would not be desirable from a military perspective. Modern military technology has made a conscript army obsolete. The fighting belly of the old army was a street-brawling roughneck or a hayseed off the farm honed to be a trench warfare soldier skilled in the old-fashioned kind of fighting—hand-to-hand combat. Contemporary warfare needs highly trained specialists and a smaller number of ground troops spearheaded by counter-insurgency units, like the Special Forces, not the masses of brave human fodder who gave their lives on Flanders Field and the Battle of the Bulge. Volunteers can fill the country's defense needs, and the military can continue to be a tough-love school for character-building for those who seek it out. Tough luck for those few, clueless, over-privileged types like me who don't bother to discover it and never grow up!

Rereading what I had written made me think what kind of person I had been and what I had become and what the army had done to change me. Mind you, we are who we are, and nothing short of a lifetime of therapy or perhaps a frontal lobotomy can really alter our basic persona. But becoming more functional, productive, happy humans living with our fellow beings in a reasonably civilized manner should be within reach for all of us. And the army certainly cut through the hocus-pocus and shrink time I most likely would have had to undergo if I had never put on a uniform. It turned me around, making me an almost totally different, much better person.

My first challenge when I joined the army was my inability to successfully defecate. The routine of basic training and living cheek-by-jowl in a barracks with a hundred other young men was a radical change for me. Even freshman year in college when I shared a suite with other undergrads, I had my own room, and the dormitory's shared bathroom facilities had individual shower and toilet stalls. No such luck at Fort Jackson, South Carolina, where I did my infantry basic training.

The latrine was a long shed with thirty commodes lined up, one next to the other, no more than twelve inches apart. When I felt my first call to nature, I was horrified to see that I would be sharing open space with dozens of other recruits for this most private of acts. I fled the place, and for six days I was in a state of increasing discomfort, unable to relieve myself. This dilemma was compounded by my not inconsiderable intake of food. Food in the army in those days was delicious and plentiful, cooked almost exclusively by Southern blacks who were master cooks, adept at serving up mouth-watering soul food. The compulsion to eat a lot in the army was caused by our hyper-activity, which demanded fuel to stoke the energy we were expending on a daily basis from dawn to dusk on forced marches and in killer calisthenics—and by boredom, the overriding *leitmotif* of military life when one was not under fire. "Hurry up and wait" was what we spent most of our time doing as recruits, and much of that time was passed standing at rigid attention with an M-1 rifle.

At last I was able to deal with the humiliation of collective defecation, and after the first successful sitting, I wondered what the big deal was all about. It was just a room with dozens of other guys doing what they had to do. And some of them did it in ways I would never have imagined and which taught me that this country was not all middle-class and suburban. I watched in total fascination when I saw a young tow-headed kid from the hills of Tennessee stand on *top* of the toilet seat and then squat down over it to perform his duty! Later when I befriended him during rifle practice, he confided to me that this was the first time in his life that he had used indoor plumbing. Stretching the truth a bit, I told him it was the same for me. It was true that on Grandma's farm, we had used an outhouse, but at least it was a sit-down privy!

Later I realized the interior design of our army latrine facilities and the resulting public nature of defecation was most probably intentional, a deliberate attempt by the army to condition us psychologically to group living and as a way to break down our individuality, which might get in the way of unquestioning obedience and the absolute adherence to following orders, even those commands that might seem stupid to us, like spit-polishing the barracks floor.

Being the consummate prevaricator that I was, I managed to get out of one of the army's most onerous duties: KP or kitchen patrol. KP entailed twelve-hour days working under tyrant cooks who kept you washing and scraping. And when you were finished doing that, there was what they called the "outside job," garbage disposal—lifting huge, heavy containers and shoveling wet garbage. At the end of a day, your hands were shriveled from hours and hours of being in dishwater. Who had heard of rubber gloves or dishwashers or disposable plates back in those good ole days!

The KP roster was in alphabetical order, and being named Oglesby had its advantages since "O" was the fifteenth letter of the alphabet. I had a few days to figure some way to weasel out of KP. I had a stash of a couple hundred dollars in my foot locker. Would a well-placed bribe be the way out of KP? Probably not. There were too many head cooks in the mess hall; whose palm to grease? If I had to make all of them happy, I would need thousands of dollars. Besides, one of them might be honest and I might end up not having KP duty but instead land in jail!

My old crutch in college for getting out of things I didn't want to do was to get a doctor's waiver. "Mr. Oglesby cannot participate in gym class due to a slipped disc." "My patient was ill on 14 November and therefore could not attend school and take his midterm examination in Statistics." It was routine for us to swing by O.K. Reed's office for any kind of excuse we needed. He was a corrupt old pill-pusher who would scribble out anything for five dollars a pop! I decided on the medical route, the only variation being that I would be the doctor!

In a moment of inspired genius, I decided that the person to approach was not in the Mess Hall, but in the Battalion Orderly Room. The fearsome Sergeant Briggs was my man! We had never spoken directly to each other, and I had avoided any personal chastisement from him. Although he certainly knew who Oglesby was, I felt sure he had not yet gotten any particular impression of me other than just being one of his lowly recruits. So far in basic training, I hadn't screwed up, or at least he hadn't noticed when I had.

Knowing that in life, timing is almost everything, I waited till what I thought was the right moment. We had a smoke break after lunch—called dinner in the army—and I approached him as he was inhaling on a Camel and watching a recruit paint the ostrich-egg-sized stones that encircled the battalion flag pole. The soldier had failed to make his bed so that the blanket was folded tight enough for a nickel bounce off it. This was a standard inspection routine in the barracks every morning, and the technique was quickly mastered, but apparently this poor sad sack painting the rocks had yet to get the hang of it.

I walked up to Briggs and saluted him, saying, "Sir, permission to speak, sir!"

Briggs replied in a surprisingly amiable way. "Spit it out, soldier. What's on your feeble mind?" Looking him straight in the eye and summonsing up the most honest expression my face could contrive, I told him I had a problem: my hands were allergic to water. No sooner had the words left my mouth than I realized I sounded preposterous. His answer was, "So what?" Thinking I had nothing to lose, I told him that my allergy gave me a problem pulling KP. To my utter surprise, he took a drag from his cigarette, turned, and walked away, saying, "I'll see what I can do about it." I never got called for KP and I never asked Sergeant Briggs what had happened. Never look a gift horse in the mouth, Grandma used to say.

With my toilet problems resolved and a mysterious exemption from KP granted, my weeks in boot camp went by quickly and I might even say enjoyably. The food was excellent, and having lost quite a few pounds in the early weeks of boot camp, I was now gaining it back as solid muscle thanks in large part to the grits and red eye, ham and black-eyed peas, and other down-home delicacies that were being cooked for us. Never being a great fan of physical activity in civilian life, I now took pleasure in serious, demanding exercise and the after effect it provided, including a good night's sleep.

The weather was cooperating, too. It was fall and neither excessively hot nor very cold. The barracks were heated with pot-bellied stoves that burned brown coal. Only towards the end of our basic training did the weather get cold enough to use these smoke-belching contraptions. In November when the weather did go down to near-freezing and the stoves were lit, a grim brown cloud hung over the camp, and inhaling the polluted air was both disagreeable and unhealthy.

Midway through boot camp, we were asked if we wanted to opt for further, advanced training. I had taken and passed a number of tests, and the choices offered me were language training at the renowned Army Language Training Center in Monterrey, California, or Officer Candidate School at Fort Benning, Georgia. Monterrey was world-famous for its beautiful location. The excellent language courses lasted two years, with one year on location in a foreign country; for Mandarin language students, a year would be spent in Taiwan. But this would mean extending my two-year enlistment by one year.

Although I was getting used to army life, I still did not relish the idea of an additional year as a grunt, especially since the Cuban missile crisis had just burst upon the world and everybody, especially those of us in uniform, were understandably nervous about the prospect of having to go to war.

One of the fatally wrong decisions of my life was made at this point, and I chose Fort Benning and OCS. Aside from not wanting to stay in the military any longer than I had to, I think, being honest with myself, I found being an enlisted man a bit distasteful. The idea of becoming an officer appealed to me as a more honorable and appropriate path for somebody like myself. After all, I was a college grad and a Virginia gentleman, wasn't I? I guess at this point I was still more of a snob than I would have admitted, and the prospect of being saluted and called Sir was a bigger deal than it should have been. There are junctures in all of our lives when we have more than one choice open to us. I often think about the road not taken and wonder what would have become of me had I chosen Monterrey.

Having made my decision, I realized there might be a problem for me in OCS. The physical requirements were extremely demanding, even more rigorous than our infantry basic training, which was saying something. Aside from accuracy in firing a weapon, at which I excelled for some strange reason, usually squatting on my haunches and looking sharp and spit-polished, the most important achievement a grunt could realize was excellence in PT (physical training) tests. Typically, the tests included feats that I could readily accomplish with ease, like push-ups and running an obstacle course, but one exercise was beyond me. It was a straight-arm hang where you had to repel yourself along a lengthy horizontal ladder for about fifty yards.

I had very painfully discovered in high school in judo practice that I had trick shoulders that would slip out of their sockets if my shoulder joints moved in a certain way and at a certain angle, and straight-arming was how it happened. I can tell you, having a shoulder go out of socket is one of the most painful experiences you can have. I had fudged on this particular exercise in basic training by either not doing it if the sergeant was not watching or by modifying the maneuvers in such a way that I got from one end of the ladder to the other even though it looked weird and I got shouted at. "Oglesby, you look like the north end of a south-bound mule! What the fuck do you think you are doin'?"

Thankfully, though I had to endure these tirades time and again, I was never asked to repeat the repel. I knew this same obstacle course would have to be faced again in OCS, only at a level of rigor and perfection far higher than what we had been doing. I now felt from my earlier KP experience with him that I must have some mystical connection with Sergeant Briggs. I was wrong. When I told him about my physical problem, he looked at me like I was a crazy white boy and said, "Oglesby, what kinda shit you talkin'?" That was that. I guessed that I would have to take my chances when I got to Fort Benning for OCS.

The day before we graduated from basic training, the battalion commander, Lt. Colonel Clifford, addressed our platoon and asked us at the end of his speech if we had any questions. Sergeant Briggs had briefed us on this appearance from on high and warned us, "If any of you sorry asses asks the colonel a question, there's gonna be hell to pay!" Risking the sergeant's wrath, I approached Colonel Clifford. He seemed to be a kindly man, rather pudgy for a battalion commander, with lots of little purple veins shooting out all over his face, the result of too much cheap commissary Bourbon over a lifetime of elbow-bending at the officers' club.

The good colonel assured me that my imagined impediment should not be an obstacle to successful completion of

OCS and wished me well. Given the limited nature of our exchange on the parade field, I did not have the chance to ask him specifically how I was going to successfully negotiate the PT requirements of OCS. Sometimes in life it is just not possible to find the right answer to an important question.

OCS was total hell. It was so bad, it was wonderful or at least our scrambled brains told us so when we roller-coastered from one manic high to another. In OCS, you never walked; you ran. When you were eating in the mess hall, there was usually a drill instructor, his nose touching yours as you fed yourself, telling you, you looked like a stupid shit and why didn't you chew that last bite twenty-two times like you were supposed to and why was your mother selling her ass on the road for ten bucks when she was only worth five. That kind of dinner conversation. They pissed me off so much that I started to fuck with them in my own way.

Once at dinner, with a DI standing over me, I dug into the food on my metal tray, eating my dessert *first*. That drove the DI crazy. He went ballistic and called the whole mess hall to attention. When ear-splitting silence had been achieved, he said, "Candidate Oglesby, perhaps you would like to enlighten the battalion as to why you are eating your dessert *before* the main course?" I replied that it looked so good, I wanted it right away. For the next hour, I got it from three DIs simultaneously. I think we all enjoyed it. The next morning I had extra laps with my rifle.

The carrot and stick philosophy was carried to an extreme at OCS. Absolutely forbidden were such delicacies as chocolate. That didn't really bother me since I had never had a sweet tooth. As a child, I had always enjoyed taking aspirins and eating large helpings of spinach when my peers were wolfing down Mars Bars. Since everything fun was forbidden, we naturally had to try to find something evil, delightful, and illegal. Sex was out of the question even though some of us, I am sure, fantasized by what we saw in the showers. So chocolate it was. The question was how to get it.

It became a challenge like a prisoner in solitary confinement scheming to get a hacksaw into his cell. The answer, as with jail birds, was wives and girlfriends. Several of the candidates had their spouses bring boxes of chocolate with them when they came for weekly visits—not conjugal visits, just "how're ya doing" encounters. Somehow the guys managed to bring the forbidden fruit back to the barracks, and when the lights were out after curfew, we turned on our flashlights and went to town on the Hersheys, gorging ourselves to distraction. Within a couple of hours, there were moans followed by loud eruptions of flatulence. But the worst was yet to come. In our sleep, most of us shit on ourselves. Memo to myself: If you're ever constipated, skip the Metamucil and eat chocolate!

Alas! Colonel Clifford's advice was not sound, and I washed out of OCS for precisely the reason I had feared. I could not negotiate the hanging bar repel, and that handicap lowered my PT score below the minimum acceptable for graduation. Halfway through the OCS course I, along with a collection of other unfortunate ex-candidates, was consigned to a barracks for wash-outs. Suddenly, we had gone from not having a spare moment in twenty-four hours to having nothing but leisure time on our hands. Now I had seen it all—going from utter distaste at the prospect of being compelled to go into the army and associate with low-types I would never have deigned to know in civilian life, to loving the army and the low-types I had met, and now to experiencing the crushing weight of total failure that had come about through no fault of my own and once again hating the army and myself to boot.

To add insult to injury, our new barracks was next to the one we had occupied as OCS candidates, and every morning while we slept in with hangovers, we could hear the roar of the battalion as it marched on the parade field, reminding us what losers we were.

The question now was, what would the army do with these undesirable wash-outs? There was rumor that some of us would be assigned to *permanent* KP. Two years of kitchen patrol. That would be a nice use of a college graduate, I told myself! Somehow after a few more weeks of doing nothing in the wash-out holding tank, I found myself moved yet again to another barracks, and during office hours—regular office hours—sitting in front of a Remington typewriter. I had become a clerk in the base personnel office. This was by no means a dream job; I would much rather have been studying Mandarin in scenic Monterrey or receiving my second lieutenant's bars in a glittering ceremony on the parade field. But here I was, and at least I was not dipping my water-allergic hands into a vat of sudsy water in some mess hall.

Life has its tiny compensations. I was amazed at my ability to adapt so readily to yet another changed set of circumstances and remain reasonably sane. I was beginning to feel that I was one tough piece of work. I had gone from being traumatized by not being able to take a shit for days on end, to reveling in the group dynamic of being in the army,

to utter failure due to few horizontal bars I could not negotiate through no fault of my own. And, catlike, I seemed to
have landed on my feet once again. I think what saved me
from being a basket case was a combination of strength of
character that, miracle of miracles, was beginning to surface
together with my basically superficial nature. I was just not
deep or sensitive enough to let anything bother me. As the
army saying goes, "Don't sweat the small stuff!" I guess, to
me, everything in life was small stuff. Was this a good attitude or not? Fifty years later, at age seventy, I'm still trying
to figure that one out!

For the next few months, life proceeded in a painless
and not unpleasant fashion. My routine desk job was not
demanding. In the evening, there were first-run movies at
the base theater for twenty-five cents and after that there was
the canteen for beers and, if one felt like it, bowling. Trips
off-base to Columbia, South Carolina, were undertaken from
time to time; we usually ended up at the University of South
Carolina, crashing some fraternity party or other. The only
problem with these forays was that Thunderbird-driving co-
eds were expensive dates, and an army private could spend
a whole month's salary in one night entertaining the self-
entitled Southern Belles who were likely to be available.

Better to stay on base and stick with what had become
my own kind. And a mixed bag it was. I especially remember one soldier with the improbable name of Fortress
Monroe. That was his real name. He was an effeminate black
guy who loved the army more than anything but was always getting in trouble for one minor infraction or another.
I suspect his real problem was his extreme flamboyance;
the army was just not ready for that kind of behavior.

Fortress Monroe was a character whose time had not yet arrived. I wondered if it ever would.

One day, Monroe just disappeared. It seems he had managed to obtain an officer's dress uniform, white linen with all of the fruit salad ribbons and decorations, and had worn this get-up to the officers' club, hoping to pass himself off as an officer and a gentleman. According to reports, he had added a touch of rouge to his face and just a hint of eye shadow to make his entrance into the club all the more dramatic. Perhaps Monroe really did think he was an officer. Private Fortress Monroe impersonating an officer! Short of murder, the one transgression in the military that is considered truly serious is to go above your rank, and impersonating an officer was an egregious offense. Monroe ended up in jail, but his love of the army never abated.

I came to realize before long that working in a personnel office was a good place to be; indeed, even as a lowly private, I was in a powerful position. With rosters of personnel in front of me and assignment options to be meted out, I had it within my power to send people to purgatory or to heaven. The choice of assignments was mind-boggling. One could end up in cushy places like Honolulu or Paris, or in hardship hellholes like Korea! A joke around the personnel office was to sing the song "Maria" from *Westside Story*, but to substitute the word Korea for Maria, as in "Korea, I just got the word it's Korea!"

Suddenly it dawned on me: what was I doing here in redneck South Carolina when I could be anywhere I wanted to send myself? With that thought in mind, I set about scanning the spread sheets for likely places where I could spend the remainder of my army career. What surfaced was interesting. It seemed that the 64th Engineer Battalion Army Map Service needed a clerk in its Teheran office. Iran! With its storybook emperor and empress, it had the reputation of being one of the nicest assignments in the army.

The 64th was an interesting operation. It was spread across Africa and the Middle East and was in the business of mapping countries. The mission even sounded altruistic: providing up-to-date maps to developing countries who did not have the means to carry out their own map-making. And a good thing it may have been for them, but the basic motive on the part of the United States was hardly altruistic. With the Cold War at its height, accurate maps were invaluable to the Americans, as was having a foothold in oil-rich countries across North Africa and the Middle East. The 64th had elements in the Kingdom of Libya, Iran, Ethiopia, and the Sudan. I wasted no time and cut a set of travel orders sending myself to the shah's paradise.

My journey to my new assignment proved that getting there is not always half the fun. We were obliged to travel via Charleston, South Carolina, Bermuda, and Morocco. Although the stopovers were not overnight, we were told to be prepared for lengthy waits and that we could be on the ground for hours and hours. What they did not tell us was that the layovers could also be brief. Bermuda and Morocco! My ears rang with the sounds of these exciting places.

I was determined to see as much as I could on these stopovers. Never mind the fact that I was an army private on a military flight and that I was, technically speaking, restricted to the airport till further notice. No sooner had we landed in Bermuda than I was out the door of the airport enjoying the sights of Hamilton. I somehow even managed to get into a pair of Bermuda shorts and take a Bermuda buggy ride. Some hours later, I decided it might be good to go back to the airport and check on our flight.

I quickly changed back into my army uniform and entered the terminal. When I reported to the flight desk, I was asked, "Soldier, where the hell have you been? Our flight has been ready to take off for Morocco for two hours, but you were *missing*! This borders on AWOL! Who the fuck do you think you are?" I sheepishly grabbed my duffel bag and joined the queue boarding the plane for Morocco. But I couldn't help laughing to myself. Here I was, a private, and I had kept the U.S. Air Force waiting for two hours. Jackie Kennedy couldn't have done better! I realized that I had been pushing my luck and could well have ended up in the "hoosegow" along with Private Fortress Monroe, but the jaws of military justice had not clamped shut on me. How many of my nine lives had I expended?

I was destined never to see the pearly gates of fabled Teheran. When the plane landed at Wheelus Air Base, Tripoli, Libya, in the Sanussi Kingdom, where there was a young lieutenant named Khaddafi still years away from his mad, murderous exploits that included the bankrolling of a plot that brought down a Pan Am jet over Lockerbie, Scotland, I was jerked off the plane and told that there had been a change of assignment orders. It seemed that the Tripoli element of the 64th needed an admin clerk and that Teheran had an over-supply of that MOS (military occupational specialty) so my trip was cut short.

My new assignment was to be Tripoli. It appeared that my reputation had proceeded me. When I had settled into the barracks and reported to the orderly room, the first sergeant, another behemoth standing about six foot five and weighing I don't know what, looked me up and down and said, "And what do we have here? A VIP, I guess. It's not every day, private, that the U.S. Air Force waits two hours for somebody! As long as you are under my command, there will be no more shenanigans. Understand?" I told him that I did, and for the rest of my stay in Libya, we got on like a house on fire. He even brought me into his office to work directly under him, preparing the morning report, that all-important daily reckoning that accounted for every soldier in the battalion, or in the case of those missing or AWOL, to report them to the military police.

This task took me approximately thirty minutes every morning. After that, I was free to do what I wished, as long as I stayed in the office. I think I became the best-read company clerk in the army since I was at leisure to peruse books and magazines all day until the night clerk came on at five o'clock. And that is what I did. Later, when I had really gained the confidence of the first sergeant, he entrusted me with a duty that was almost sacred to him. He allowed me to feed his Venus Fly Trap, a carnivorous plant that sat on his desk and consumed flies, hamburger, and anything else we could find to feed it. As long as I kept Lucy happy, first sergeant was copasetic.

My experience with the army in Libya began to show me how insular most Americans were when they lived overseas. Wheelus Air Base was a gigantic piece of real estate constructed to resemble a small American town, complete with all of the amenities of suburban life: movie theaters, a bowling alley, shops, a hospital, and houses for the dependent families of enlisted and officer-rank personnel. Nobody seemed to have the slightest interest in exploring what lay outside the airbase gates.

I quickly grew tired of this circumscribed environment, and at every opportunity, I took off for Tripoli, exploring its souks and cafes and the rich life that was a mixture of Arab, Italian, and ancient Jewish cultures. Libya had been part of the Ottoman Empire until 1919, when it was transferred to one of the victors of the First World War, Italy, to become an Italian colony until 1945. I was fascinated with the fusion of cultures and languages one encountered on the streets of Libya, and I gradually made friends with expatriates and locals whom I encountered.

I became especially close to one couple, an Englishman and his French wife. They had an infant son, and I used to baby-sit for them on weekends. It gave me the chance to get away from the barracks, which was in a horrid location near the base gates where braying camels and indescribable odors were a constant annoyance. I found another soldier who had managed to buy an ancient VW from somebody for almost nothing, and we took weekend excursions to the magnificent Roman ruins of Sabratha and Leptis Magna.

I also took advantage of the incredible network MATS flights that would allow anybody in uniform to hitchhike wherever he pleased. During my time in Libya, I managed to make trips to Malta, Naples, London, Glasgow, and Paris. Not bad for a private in the U.S. army! I made some good army friends whom I would see later in my life in places as scattered as Vietnam and Washington DC. I found the camaraderie that tied us grunts together was a powerful bond that would allow us to pick up when we saw each other years later and carry on as though we had never parted ways.

One of my last memories of Libya was also one of my saddest. It was November 22, 1963, and I was alone in the barracks, relaxing on my bunk listening to Armed Forces radio around 5:00 p.m., if I recall. The other troops had gone off to a softball game, and it was good to be alone for a change. Through a half-doze, I heard an announcement over the radio that seemed to say that President Kennedy had been shot in Dallas, Texas. I bolted up and listened carefully and the news was repeated.

I rushed to the orderly room, where the duty officer and a couple of his cronies were playing poker. As I burst through the door, I shouted, "President Kennedy has been shot." Four pairs of eyes looked up from their cards at me, and one soldier said with an exasperated tone in his voice, "Oglesby's trying to be funny again. You college grads have the weirdest sense of humor. That just ain't funny!" It took more than a few minutes to convince them that what I was saying was true. I finally did so by leading them into the barracks where the news was being repeated on the radio.

Several months later, I said my good-byes to the 64th and made my way to the Swiss Alps, where I had taken a job teaching at a boarding school in Leysin, Switzerland. I was a month shy of being twenty-five years old and had already had more than my share of experiences. Others were to follow.

As I stepped into my low-quarter civilian shoes and walked out the Battalion Headquarters gate, I felt my heart leap and my ankles wobble. I realized that I had become "boot dependent." For two years I had worn heavy combat boots laced tightly up to mid-calf. My ankles had become used to the total support that Army footwear had provided. Now I was on my own, but my ankles weren't so sure they could make it. It would take a few weeks walking up hills in Switzerland before I really felt liberated from the Army!

[CHAPTER FOUR]

JAIL CELL WITH A VIEW
The Swiss Alps Never Looked So Bad

In the final weeks of my military service—that would have been late summer, 1964—I began thinking about what I wanted to do with my life. I was twenty-four years-old, had a rather limp "gentleman's C" bachelor's degree in liberal arts from the University of Virginia, and not much ambition. I entertained the vague idea that maybe I wanted to return to the Eastern Shore of Maryland and go into farming ... or did I want to go to Paris and study French? As a low-ranking enlisted man, decision-making had not been a habit I was used to. Quite the contrary, at my level, the military encouraged unquestioning obedience in favor of independent thinking, and I had zoned out at that point in my life when I should have been developing my A-type juices.

I had managed to finish my two years as a draftee in the army without major calamity—I had not picked up a serious drinking habit as many of my grunt peers had done—and found myself about to become a civilian— "reentering the world," in military parlance—with good prospects of an honorable discharge and a few hundred dollars in my pocket. What to do? I had spent the second half of my army assignment, one year, in what was then the Kingdom of Libya as a corporal attached to the 64th Engineer Battalion, U.S. Army Map Service. By process of elimination, I could immediately rule out staying in Libya. There were no job prospects there for foreigners who did not have expertise in oil exploration—Libya was just starting to come into its own as a major petroleum producer—and after twelve months in an arid country with a rather closed society—closed at least to young, non-Arab-speaking Westerners—a future there did not present exciting prospects.

My duties with the 64th had been light, to say the least, and consisted of various administrative tasks, the shuffling of paper. During those final days in uniform, I spent most of my time in the back recesses of Battalion Headquarters, squirreled away at a desk buried behind rolls of maps we had been making. My major pursuit besides drinking gallons of weak army coffee and teasing Ali, the fifty-year-old Libyan cleaning "boy" and bantering with Cox, a red neck ole boy from Tennessee, was reading the *New York Times* European edition and the *International Herald Tribune*, which I used to pick up at the mess hall every morning and read backwards and forwards by noon each day. I was also in an Evelyn Waugh period, devouring almost all of his books, at least the ones that did not deal with his ponderous conversion to Catholicism. The volume that delighted me most was *Vile Bodies*, Waugh's mad-cap account of a twenty-something teaching at an eccentric boarding school for over-privileged brats of the English aristocracy.

One morning, a classified ad on the back page of the *International Herald Tribune* caught my eye. A boarding school in Leysin, Switzerland, was advertising for a high school history teacher starting September 1964. That was two weeks away, a few days before I terminated my army gig. I went into the orderly room, and Sergeant Major Paul told me I could get an early release from the army if I had a job to go to. I then raced back to the barracks and dug into my locker and fished out my Brooks Brothers jacket, a white dress shirt, and a tie and went out the base gate to an Italian photographer to pose for a job application photograph.

The result, which I received the following day, showed what looked like a rather stern disciplinarian with a close-cropped military hair cut and a "don't mess with me" look in his eye. I dashed back to my desk and typed out a resume that scarcely filled one page, together with a cover letter, and mailed it to the Leysin American School, Canton de Vaud, Leysin, Switzerland, Attention: Dr. Jose Gonzalez, Headmaster. Within days, I received a reply accepting me as LAS's new history teacher! The contract was for one year and included room and board as well as a rather modest salary in Swiss francs. I laughed to myself as I tucked the letter into the almost finished volume of *Vile Bodies*. At LAS would there be a Mrs. Best-Chetwynd with a Rolls Royce and a Negro boyfriend named Chokie? Would I have impossible students like the bespectacled Piggie? As it turned out, there would be that and more!

Duly demobilized and wearing my trusty Brooks Brothers jacket instead of an army monkey suit, I shook hands, with great satisfaction, with the officers who had commanded me instead of giving them a grovelly salute, conspicuously omitting "Sir" when I bid them farewell. Within hours, I was boarding a sleek little Caravelle jet that would take me from Tripoli to Lausanne, Switzerland, for the next chapter in my life.

After several connections—taxi, bus, and rail—I arrived at the hamlet of Aigle on the eastern tip of Lake Geneva from where I boarded a toylike mountain train with cog wheels that climbed steeply for forty-five minutes to the mountain village of Leysin. The hills on both sides of the railway track were covered with orderly rows of vineyards. Leysin was in the Canton de Vaud, which was famous for its white wine called *fendant*. Over the next year, my teacher colleagues and I would imbibe many bottles of this delightful, slightly bubbly liquid and sample other varieties, including the full-bodied red *Dole*. It was going to be a liquid year.

Although demobilized, the army was still with me in the form of my duffel bag, a long tubelike piece of canvas luggage into which I had crammed all my worldly possessions.

Digging out what I wanted was a challenge since packing a duffel bag involved squeezing and pressing in dozens of layers to fit everything into the long container before securing it with a heavy padlock. Even locking it did not guarantee security, as I had discovered back in the barracks when I saw a buddy's bag slashed open, with its contents spilling out like the innards of a bleeding calf. Switzerland was famous for its cuckoo clocks and chocolate and also, I was told, its honesty, so I was not worried about the safety of my modest collection of possessions as I panted and climbed up the road for the half-mile walk from the train station to my new home, the Leysin American School.

Due to advances in medical technology, Leysin and other picturesque mountain villages in the Swiss Alps had undergone a major transformation over the past thirty years. Having originally flourished as spas catering to tuberculosis patients at a time when sunshine and rest were deemed the best cures for this insidious disease, the advent of medication had rendered these picturesque locales obsolete for those seeking the cure. So it was that Leysin and its likes slipped into the doldrums, becoming pastoral backwaters until after the Second World War, when post-war prosperity brought skiers and beautiful people to the slopes for sport and après-ski. The empty shells that had been TB clinics found new life in the form of hotels and boarding schools for children of the affluent. Diplomats in hardship assignments and overseas businessmen, mostly oil drillers in Saudi Arabia, were eager to find convenient, not-too-distant locations for schooling their children, as were jet-setters who preferred to dump Junior somewhere so they could get on with their Mexican divorces and other lifestyle requirements that were hindered by the presence of pesky children.

These old clinics were stately, stolid, and not unattractive buildings, always pleasantly perched on a hillside—*bâti sur un beau rivage*—from where postcard-perfect alpine views and pure rays of cancer-inducing sunshine were to be had in great supply. Even tarted up with optimistic shades of paint on the classroom walls and chintz-covered sofas in the school reception area, sly reminders that the ghost of the Grim Reaper was still with us were to be found in the overly commodious elevators, which had been designed to accommodate coffins, and in a gigantic area that had served as the sanatorium clinic. This was now the school health station, overseen by a bodacious, blonde English nurse. She wore a peaked cap and a crisp, white uniform that crackled and rustled as she glided among the gleaming glass medicine cabinets, glancing at her wristwatch and making the occasional adjustment to her plunging décolletage.

The mountain panorama across the valley was truly stunning, and my school colleagues often waxed poetic about how they couldn't start their day without pausing to meditate on this splendor. As for myself, having admired them once from the balcony of my room on the second floor of the boys' dormitory, I seemed never to notice those elegant, snow-capped peaks again over the next twelve months. Not that they weren't drop-dead beautiful; it was just that they were there, something to be taken for granted and therefore ignored. Even beauty can become routine and dull if it is around you in overabundance. No wonder Mount Rainier in Seattle, Washington, is so popular. She has the good sense to emerge from mist and clouds only one day in three throughout the year.

My accommodation at the school was Spartan, to say the least. Aside from teaching, one of the "extra" duties sprung upon me was to be dormitory monitor for the senior highschool-aged boys. This meant living on the same floor with them, sharing their bathroom, and making sure that the Beatles were not blaring at night when they were supposed to be doing their homework. I was also detailed to morning inspection to ensure that beds were made and belongings tidied away in ship-shape order and that telltale whiffs of cigarette smoke were not present.

Inspection stickers were affixed to each door, and each room was rated with the appropriate box checked for neatness or lack thereof. The worst possible category was a "See Me!" which appeared at the bottom of the sheet. I don't think I ever used that one. Before long, the boys were saying, "Mr. O is a push-over. He never really checks out our rooms." Perhaps I was too easy, and maybe the headmaster, Dr. Gonzalez, had been deceived by the military mien in my application photograph. On reflection, that picture was probably what got me hired. But from my standpoint, I had had enough of things military, and besides, adding these extra duties exposed me to the kids 24/7, which was not in my contract. Who wanted to stand in line behind a screeching band of pubescent fifteen-year-olds and wait an eternity to shower? Had I not had enough of "hurry up and wait" in the army?

Surprisingly, and contrary to my expectations, the students were, on the whole, a good lot of kids, not the bunch of self-entitled, over-privileged little snots I had anticipated. There were several who required watching, but there was no drug problem, not even smoking or alcohol consumption, and I would have known if there had been. I managed to establish a special relationship with a cunning, homely senior named Jim.

We had a tidy understanding where we both used each other in a mutually advantageous arrangement. Jim, as an unabashed informant, would rat on fellow students if he thought there was something I should know about, and, in exchange, I turned my head to the excessive stash of consumable goodies he kept in his room. Reminiscent of the hoarding wheeler-dealer sergeant in *Stalag 17*, he had a closet that spilled over with boxes of chocolates, biscuits, soda pop, and other forbidden delicacies, which he used to bribe various staff members and fellow students, and, on occasion, me. In time, I become the kind of teacher who was thought of as the students' pal, a far cry from what the good Dr. Gonzalez had hired me for. In that capacity, I came to know more gossip about the student body than even the wily Jim was privy to.

For example, I was aware that two fresh-faced sophomores were regularly stand-up screwing in the linen closet next to the staff kitchen. The school was co-ed with two floors of boys' dorms and two levels for the girls, seemingly well-separated by the main floor of the school, which housed classrooms and the school library. The only hitch was, incredible as it may seem, the sole English language dictionary in the entire school was to be found in the library, and the rule was it could not be removed from its stand. Nobody ever used it except Russell and Hortense, a pair of nerdy fifteen-year-olds, and they seemed to need to search the meaning of words on a nightly basis. My sleuthing discovered that they both got permission from the dorm monitors on their respective floors to go to the library after 9:00 p.m., when it had already closed, to look up words.

From there, they made a beeline to a floor below to the linen closet for a good fifteen-minute bang and then returned to their dorms, no one being the wiser. After I found out about these nightly workouts, I avoided direct confrontation with Russell; instead, I started joking with him about his love of dictionaries and his devotion to spelling words right. His self-conscious snickers told me I was on the right track. Next, risking a flurry of village gossip

("*Tu sais, Marie, le jeune prof là-bas a l'école Américaine? Hier il a acheté un tas de capotes! Figure-toi! Qu'est-ce que se passe avec ces étrangers dan notre village de Leysin!*-Hey, Marie, you know that young professor up at the American school? Yesterday he bought a bunch of rubbers! What are all those foreigners doing to our village!"), I proceeded to the local pharmacy after classes one afternoon and bought a pack of condoms.

The next time I ran into Russell, I waved him aside and pulled him into a corner, dangling the packet of protectives in front of his nose. Rhetorically, I asked him, "Russell, do you know what these are for?" and slipped them into his pocket. He blushed a deep crimson, and as I walked away, I left him with the admonishment, "Use 'em!" Since I did not see any balloons inflated in the dorm over the coming days, I assumed Russell had put them to good use, thereby avoiding the school's first in-house pregnancy. I saw nothing wrong with my seemingly permissive treatment of Russell, although I am sure had these trysts been known to Dr. G and company, there would have been inquiries, accusations, and perhaps even firings and dismissals. I figured letting nature take its course was not only realistic but, in this case, educative. After all, my father told me he had been seduced by an older woman when he was twelve and he was none the worse for it. Although a semi-virgin at age twenty-four and not very steeped in the ways of the world myself, I was proud of the rather sophisticated French attitude I had adopted.

Despite its youthful population, the surrounding glory of the Swiss Alps and the picture-perfect postcard village, the school somehow seemed a somber place. I reflected on this downer of an environment and decided it was because we were in Switzerland—orderly, hardworking, and rather boring, or as our school French teacher, Madame de la Suda, loved to say, "*Ah, La Suisse*- quatre *cent ans de paix et l'horloge cuckoo*!*-Ah*, Switzerland, four hundred years of peace and the cuckoo clock!" The one ray of joy and light in our staid institution were the Spanish workers who toiled in the kitchen and performed other menial tasks too lowly for the peace-loving Swiss.

They worked back-breaking seven-day weeks and were only given a respite on Sunday afternoons, when they all gathered in the school courtyard for a riotous marathon of volleyball, dancing, and singing. Loaded down with hampers of Spanish sausage, paella, and bottles of *tinto*, they sang and laughed the afternoon away, and the strange sound of happiness and joy filled the chilly mountain air. I always attended these gatherings if I could, positioning myself discreetly on the sidelines so as not to intrude on their precious window of leisure when they could uninhibitedly be their Spanish selves. But they would have none of it, dragging me into their midst to share their food, wine, and laughter. We had no language in common, but I discovered the best communication is often without words.

I started noticing at these weekly gatherings a collection of LAS students, an assortment of what I frankly viewed as the least attractive members of our student body—overweight, pimply, whining mediocrities who were always trying to disrupt class with stupid, attention-getting pranks that nobody appreciated. The leader of this group was a pasty-faced, obese sixteen-year-old named Franz who came from somewhere in Ohio. He had been sent to the school by his father, who worked as an oil rig hog somewhere in the

Persian Gulf. I had had several run-ins with Franz, as had other members of the faculty.

The head of the Physical Education Department, John Harland, a world-class mountain climber, had harshly disciplined him once in front of other students, reducing him to blubbering jelly and relieving him of any smidgen of self-respect he may have had. This propelled Franz to pick on people he felt were weaker and more vulnerable than he was, and his new target was the hard-working, happy Spaniards. Standing on the sidelines of the volleyball court, he and his hapless cohorts began chanting what sounded like *"Grease!"*

At first, I thought they might be cheering the players on, but then I realized what they were doing. They were demeaning the hardworking kitchen staff by insulting them. Luckily, a language barrier prevented the target of these insults from understanding the nasty word being flung at them. They simply smiled and continued to sing and play, which seemed to infuriate the miscreants who were taunting them. I approached them and told them to move on. At first, they mumbled that it was Sunday and they could do whatever they wanted. I somehow managed to muster a bit of my military toughness and told them to move out and make it quick. They ambled on, tossing a few more insults back at the Spaniards.

The next week, they appeared again at the volleyball game and resumed their nasty tirade. This time, one of them had brought a megaphone. The Spaniards now seemed to understand the meaning of what was being hurled at them. With heads bowed, they stopped their game, picked up their equipment and their uneaten food, and walked away. Some of them were openly weeping. I was wracked with grief over what had happened and frantically tagged behind as they left, assuring them with my few words of Spanish that "*no es nada.*" They were not to be consoled and never again returned on Sundays to spread happiness to our somber campus. I heard that they had found another place in the village, a playing field at the local Swiss middle school where they could have their Sunday gatherings. Not long after that, Franz left the school, and his skinhead movement seemed to evaporate. But sadly, whenever I met the Spaniards, they were distant to me, perhaps thinking that, after all, a *gringo* is a *gringo*.

The other staff were indeed a mixed bag. There was Frau Mainz, manager of the school's kitchen and surely the original prototype for a concentration camp matron. Sixty-ish with iron gray hair and a bulldog face, she was infamous for her standard statement, blurted out in German-accented English, "Ya, but I have my orders!" As watch dog of the three meals served every day, she had been given instructions from the school's board of directors to keep expenses down at all costs and economize on food, which was seen as the most important variable in the school overhead where more profit could be realized. This meant the smallest of portions with no second helpings at mealtime and a diet that was characterized mainly by starch and cabbage.

Once interrogated about the watery nature of her chicken soup, Frau Mainz responded to her challengers by producing a tureen of the suspect liquid and ladling out a portion into a soup bowl. When no meat appeared, she indignantly declared, "Ya, but I saw a piece of chicken when it was in the kitchen! Where is it, dat chicken? Where is it!" Throughout the first semester, there was raging controversy over whether the students could have an afternoon snack, something to tide them over between lunch at one o'clock and dinner at six thirty. Growing adolescents who participated in vigorous sports had nagging appetites by late afternoon, and Frau Mainz was confronted on a daily basis about providing something to fill their stomachs. After threat of a strike by the student body, she gave in and, at the appointed time every day after gym class, the students single-filed in the dining room to be handed a shriveled apple.

Juxtaposed to Frau Mainz were the Swiss ladies in the laundry room who meticulously washed and ironed our clothing. Payday for the teachers happened every two weeks when we signed for cash and walked away, pockets bulging with francs. Once I managed to lose my fortnightly salary and wondered how I was going to survive till next payday. When I went to pick up my laundry two days later, Doris, the cheerful washer woman, handed over my sack of clothes and quietly whispered to me , "And there's this, too!" pressing a wad of money into my hand. It was the missing salary I had absentmindedly left in my dirty trousers.

Our dormitory hallway and bathrooms were cleaned by Michel, a fortyish man from Poland with a high-pitched, nervous voice. Michel was easily agitated over anything, and the boys quickly caught on to this tick and teased him incessantly. Sometimes three of them would back Michel into a corner and tickle him in the ribs. At six feet, he towered over these children but remained totally defenseless when confronted with such horseplay. The terrified look on his face and his blood-curdling screams caused me to run out of my room one day, and as he wildly waved his arms at the boys, I saw the tattooed numbers inked on his forearm.

Although, strictly speaking, she was staff, the school nurse, Delia, hung out with the teachers. In her twenties and very attractive, she seemed frustrated that she had landed in a place where there was no male talent to her liking. Aside from the students who were too young—although I did catch her in the middle of a heavy flirt with one of the handsome older boys in the infirmary once—there were no eligibles. The Spaniards were *infradig*, the Swiss too clannish, and the other faculty members either married, queer, or beyond the pale of age and acceptable looks. So Delia spent a lot of her time telling the females on staff about Franco and her other Italian lovers, who were, alas, in faraway Naples or Rome.

I was not interested in Delia romantically, but I found her nice and once lent her what for me was a good deal of money, the equivalent of a month's salary. All done over a handshake and a smile, she completely forgot I had lent her money and that she had not paid me back. When I asked her six months later to repay me, she took offense, denying that she hadn't made good on her debt, and then grudgingly handed over the cash and never spoke to me again. Memo to myself: bad form as it may be, always write a note and sign it when money is involved.

The faculty was divided into two camps: the old-timers, who had been there for years, and the bright young things *a la* Evelyn Waugh, who had come to teach for a year or two and have a Swiss adventure. Leading the old-timer camp was Ludmila, the Russian teacher whom I nicknamed the Old Bolshevik. She had been there for ages and accused all of us of picking on her because she was Russian. It was a baseless accusation since hardly anybody spoke to her.

Obviously she wanted attention and was frustrated at being overlooked in the dining room during meals, the only time we saw her. She ended up bonding with Dr. Gonzalez's wife, Matusha, and once, concealed behind a potted palm in *Les Orchidées* tea room, I heard them confide to each other about their preferred sexual positions and what a woman of a certain age did about "dryness." I distinctly remember hearing Matusha's solution to that problem when she whispered the word "Butter!" to the old Bolshie.

At a distance from all of us was Miss Oldcorn from Bath, on the brink of middle-age and blessed with a classic peaches-and-cream English complexion. Had she not been so old-maidish, Miss Oldcorn could have had her pick of *beaux* if there had been any. Bright, rather charming, and well-spoken, with her standard received pronunciation and round tones, the only defect in her otherwise lithe and hourglass figure were grossly oversized calves that belonged more to a hippo than a human. On the advice of Delia, Miss O switched to slacks and pantsuits, but not before the students had glimpsed her oversized gams and bestowed upon her the nickname that only adolescent cruelty can devise: Legs. I had my own nickname for Miss Oldcorn – The Iron Maiden – due to her rather steely, inflexible personality.

"Hot Dog" Sommers was self-appointed leader of the young things. A Bible-quoting holier-than-thou twit, he was, with his blonde pompadour, the spitting image of matinee idol Troy Donahue and was fond of telling us how the author James Baldwin had once flirted with him, simultaneously revealing his homophobia and his self-preoccupation. I never liked him from the get-go and heartily hated him after an encounter on the slopes my first day of skiing when he told me, "Don't break your neck." Years later, I saw him in the UN offices in Dhaka, Bangladesh, where I was assigned, and had the satisfaction of looking him straight in the face and pretending that I didn't know him.

Then there was Dr. Jose Gonzalez, our headmaster. Florid-faced and bombastic, he claimed to be an opera singer and would organize musical soirees at the school where he would bleat out arias in a voice depleted by alcohol and tobacco. His disappointment with me was instantaneous. At the first school orientation when faculty were introduced to the student body, he pointed to me and announced that "with Mr. Oglesby fresh from the military, I am sure we will have no disciplinary problems here at the Leysin American School. Isn't that right, Mr. Oglesby?"

Failing miserably to take his cue, I responded with a meek giggle and a shrug and said, "I don't know." As he rolled his eyes, I realized that any chance of a contract renewal was nil.

Several months into the school term, the assistant headmaster, an ambitious American named Frank Lanza, abruptly resigned. We speculated that the lack of personal chemistry between him and Dr. G had led to his being canned, but the problem went deeper than that. Months later, it was revealed that the headmaster had been creaming funds from the school treasury, inflating tuition costs and pocketing the difference and playing games with his income tax, and that Lanza had confronted him and had been fired. Before long, the school was rudderless when Dr. Gonzalez himself was apprehended and placed under arrest. He was later sent to a jail in Aigle, which was a stone's throw from the tracks of the little mountain train that cranked its way to Leysin every day. It was said that if passengers opened their windows and leaned out, they could hear a catarrhal voice belting out plaintive arias from Italian operas. It was Dr. Gonzalez singing to the world from his jail cell.

【CHAPTER FIVE】

SAIGON OY!
Oh, What a Lovely War It Was

Flying higher than it normally would have to avoid enemy anti-aircraft fire, our little twin-engine Air America Dornier bobbed giddily through puffs of clouds, pointing itself due south along Route 13 towards Saigon's Ton Son Nhut Airport. As I looked out the window thousands of feet to the red ribbon of road below, I thought how strange were the ways of aeronautics; the exact opposite tactic was true for helicopters: to avoid enemy fire, choppers flew low, so low they almost touched the ground. I remembered many helicopter rides where we were skimming along so close to the rice paddies, I thought we would knock the rice farmers' heads off. Well, for me those joy rides were all over now.

Our airplane's bobbing and jouncing was caused by its lightness; there were only two passengers, me and Sergeant Dobbs, and no cargo except for several large, empty Styrofoam chests that were destined to be filled with dry ice and T-bone steaks from the big commissary in Saigon and then flown back to the 1st Division field kitchen bivouacked on the edge of the Terres Rouges rubber plantation outside An Loc, my up-country duty station for over one year. These airborne supply runs for steaks, booze, and other goodies were routine provisioning exercises.

Not exactly the kind of use of aircraft I would have envisaged in a war that was touted as being a counter-insurgency, but at this point, my disillusionment with the Vietnam War was so profound that almost nothing would have surprised or shocked me. If there were regular helicopter runs to bring hot pizzas to the grunts in the field—never mind that the enemy carried tiny pouches of cold, cooked rice that had to last them for days—why not ferry a few boxes of air-mailed steaks to keep the Big Red One happy? The war was going to hell in a hand basket, but at least our troops were getting some good eats. Better to die with your stomach full of comfort food than to perish with a belly full of K-rations.

Air-delivered grub was not the only thing that troubled me. I had also been bowled over by what was happening in the villages surrounding the Big Red One's encampment area. Shacks with signs over the door, like "Big Mama's" and "House of Blue Lights" had sprung up. Hanging out the windows of these make-shift structures were rouged-up village girls, who months earlier had been bending over ir-rigated rows planting rice. Now their twelve-year-old broth-ers were pimping for them. "Hey, GI, you wanna fuck my sister? She got hot pussy! Ten dollah! I got condom! No baby, no problem!"

My time in Nam was about over, and thus far it seemed that I might actually make it out of this sad, wonderful coun-try alive. I prayed my luck would hold out a few more days. I had survived hundreds of helicopter rides over dicey territory, sometimes being fired on. And our encampment in An Loc, which was a sitting duck for enemy attack, had so far never been assaulted. We knew they were out there by the thousands, but for some reason, Charlie chose not to attack us, at least not yet. The French plantation, with its tens of thousands of mature rubber trees providing a protective canopy, was home to the NVA (North Vietnamese Army) as well as the local Viet Cong. We knew all hell would break loose one of these days—the only question was when. It was February 1968, and I was headed to Saigon for a few days of debriefing and then back to Washington DC, where I would formally terminate my career with the State Department and begin another chapter in my life.

The Vietnamese new year, Tet, was approaching, and I was glad to leave An Loc, the small town where I had been assigned for the past year working in what we called "pacification" programs. Today what we were doing would be called "nation-building"; both terms were alternate la-bels for counter-insurgency, the attempt to win over the lo-cal population's hearts and minds by providing them with things that would presumably give them a better life, aim-ing to create conditions that would give the Vietnamese a government that was responsive to their needs.

The upstream element of these programs focused on orchestrating free and fair elections and stamping out corruption, putting in place something that could compete with what Ho Chi Minh had devised for winning the allegiance of so many of his countrymen. But with a war raging, we were now more concerned with less lofty endeavors, which included providing large quantities of rice, powdered milk, and tin roofing to villagers whose homes and livelihoods had been destroyed by the insurgent Viet Cong and North Vietnamese Army or by the "friendlies"—the U.S .military and their counterparts, the ARVN, or Army of Vietnam.

During the week-long Tet festivities, a truce had been arranged between the warring factions and it was expected that both sides would lay down their guns for at least a few days. What replaced the pause in gunfire was almost as bad. Powerful firecrackers imported from China were being ignited practically non-stop night and day, with little or no regard for safety. How ironic it would be, I thought, if some of us were injured or killed by a firecracker in the midst of this senseless war—not unlike the neighbor on the farm next to ours back in Maryland who had fought gallantly in the trenches on the Western front in World War I only to be run over and killed by a tractor on his own property once he had gotten safely home.

As I packed my few belongings, shaking out my clothing to rid it of the red dust that covered everything in our compound, I felt we Americans were becoming a laughing stock and that our well-intentioned efforts were not only failing but were feeding into the corrupt system that had given the enemy cause for success. Our main preoccupation, the distribution of commodities, had been sabotaged with the meddling of the province chief's wife, the corrupt, corpulent Ba Trung Ta. Soon after our trucks delivered tin roofing and rice to the villagers, a Vietnamese army lorry would be dispatched to collect these same goods, which would then be sold back to the villagers for an exorbitant price, the proceeds being pocketed by Madame Province Chief.

What to do? Since we were guests of the Vietnamese government and white foreigners, our hands were tied insofar as dictating what could and could not be done by the Vietnamese authorities to their own people. The Vietnamese had thrown out the French colonialists a few years earlier for being meddlers. We were told by our bosses in Saigon and Washington to tread softly and not make the same mistakes that earlier white men had made. We were the easy Americans.

But even in areas where we could control what was happening, we seemed to be dithering and inept. The example that rankled me the most was the misuse of the Air America flights that serviced our province. Each day, one or two planes would arrive in An Loc from Saigon, bringing mail and passengers who were official visitors. Almost always, the plane would return to Saigon half empty. Since road travel to the capital was said to be insecure with the Viet Cong setting up roadblocks and stopping buses to collect taxes from passengers and even kidnapping the wealthier ones, a seat on an airplane was a prize worth a high price.

Somehow word got out that the Americans were allowing Vietnamese civilians to travel on our aircraft on a first-come-first-served basis. Overnight, our office turned into an airline booking agency, and our staff were swamped with requests for seats on the planes. Every morning when I would arrive at the office, I had a hard time getting to my desk due to the crowds of people beseeching me to let them travel to visit a sick relative, to go to Saigon for emergency medical treatment ... whatever. Then there were the flocks of young lovelies who said they were the province chief's sisters.

I knew perfectly well that nearly all of these requests were bogus and that the passengers were traveling for reasons that had nothing to do with helping Vietnam. Once the flood gates were opened, there was no turning back. By refusing to allocate those empty seats to the population, we would appear to be mean, the last thing we wanted in our campaign to win their hearts and minds. But by acceding to their requests, we were perverting our mission and becoming nothing more than two-bit travel agents diverting our staff and resources away from more legitimate concerns.

As our Dornier descended through the bumpy air pockets over Saigon, I found myself in a state of mind most succinctly described by that old army acronym that grunts shouted as they stepped off the plane returning to civilian life: "FIGMO"—fuck it, got my orders (orders for demobilization, that is). Let the poor souls back in An Loc deal with the province chief's "sisters" and all of the other shit that was swirling around them and, for God's sake, let's hope that Tet doesn't turn into a blood bath with those Commie fuckers violating the truce.

I thought of the few friends I had made who were still back there. My roommate, Brian. He was an ex-Peace Corps volunteer, and we had become good friends even though he had given me the bad habit of waking up at three every morning to indulge in a huge snack that would usually result in wasting a whole leg of lamb or a can of ham. He had hoped to bring some of the grassroots approaches he had applied in his village work in Nepal to "winning hearts and minds" in Vietnam, but with Madame Province Chief calling the shots, there was slim likelihood he would succeed.

Then there was Lieutenant Mike. We had been army buddies years before when we were grunts together in the 64th Engineer Battalion in Libya. I had put army life behind me, but Mike had stayed in and had gone to Officer Candidate School and was now a lifer. One day a Jeep roared into our compound in An Loc in a cyclone of red dust, and who stepped out but Lieutenant Mike, "Flaps" to me. I had given him that nickname back in Libya because his ears were so large and Dumbo-like that it looked like if he flapped them enough that he could take off and fly. Mike was based in the high-danger zone with the Big Red One, the 1st Infantry Division on the edge of the rubber plantation out at Quan Loi. When Charlie got ready to rumble, it would be Mike and his guys who would get hit first.

With his access to the army's heavy equipment, we had cadged Mike into helping us with some civil works projects with the promise that we would treat him to all the margaritas he could drink when the job was done. The officers' quarters clown was Joel Goldberg, a Brooklyn boy who was a captain in army intelligence. Every month his mother would send him, via the good offices of the APO-Army Post Office, a huge smoked salmon. Towards the end of the month, the fumes from the carcass of this smelly fish would drive us to distraction while Joel waxed poetic over the beauty of Brooklyn deli delights.

That was our group. Dedicated, decent people who were trapped in a war that had no business being fought and whose end we could not envisage. As evenings wore on and alcohol flowed, we used to ask ourselves, "How is this fucking war gonna end?" We always concluded we had no idea what the denouement would be. But, as it turned out, seven years later in 1975, the ending was far simpler than we could have imagined. The North Vietnamese simply pushed south and one day ended up smashing through the gates of Independence Palace in Saigon with their tanks and, suddenly, it was over. But that was light years away, and there were still many mistakes to be made and millions of lives to be lost before it all ended.

Although I had been living and working in An Loc for over a year, I was allowed to keep an apartment in Saigon as sort of a *pied-a-terre* for R &R visits to the city. The accommodation provided me was a luxury flat in a leafy section of town, fully accessorized with expensive Danish modern furniture. It even included a winsome Vietnamese housekeeper named Bai whose winking and smiling gave me the feeling that she was interested in more than sweeping. The whole idea of having this deluxe apartment made my head spin. Here we were, fighting a war against an enemy who rode bicycles down the Ho Chi Minh trail, lived off the land, and survived on a fistful of cold rice once a day. And what were we doing? Spending big bucks on apartments that were only used a couple of days a month and running a phony airline so that provincial swells could bring their mistresses up from Saigon for the weekend.

At this point, I had become adept at dismissing reality, so I forgot about all of this senseless shit when I came to Saigon and tried to enjoy myself in this delightful city. The only problem with my apartment was Kurt. It was a spacious two-bedroom flat, so the embassy housing office had decided to pair me up with a roommate, especially since I was seldom in town. They selected a middle-aged bachelor who worked in the film department of the U.S. Information Agency. Kurt was a naturalized American of German extraction who had been a soldier in Hitler's army and who had been captured by the United States and sent to POW camp in Texas in 1943 while the war was still raging in Europe.

In a booming voice with a *katzenjammer* accent, Kurt regaled me with stories about how he was put to work on a farm and how he was fucking Texas farmers' daughters whose husbands were getting shot at in the Battle of the Bulge. Ha ha ha! It was all a big joke, he said. Usually his farmer war stories would be interrupted by the arrival of Dung, his girlfriend, who had an ear-splitting cackle and who wore a pound of pancake makeup on her face. Her routine was unvaried. She would suddenly appear in the living room, opening the front door with her own key, and proceed to the bedroom, where she would ceremoniously sit on Kurt's king-sized mattress and bounce up and down, screeching, "Kurt, come and get me!" By the time Kurt moved into our apartment, I think his ardor for Dung was waning. She would bounce and shriek, and Kurt would ignore her, preferring to continue talking to me about those halcyon Texas days.

On this final trip to Saigon, I would be spared the rantings of Kurt and the screeching of Dung. I had given up my share in the flat and had settled in for these last few days in a seedy hotel in the center of town. Hotel de la Paix had certainly seen better days, as had its owner, a shriveled Corsican wheeler-dealer of indeterminate age whose conniving face had been jaundiced by years of opium smoking. Monsieur Secchi led me to what was surely the darkest, mustiest room I had ever rented and stared at me with milky eyes before saying, "If there's anything else you want, I can get it for you."

Since I already knew and enjoyed Saigon from dozens of trips over the past year, I disappointed him with a terse, *"Merci, mais j'ai mes propres tuyaux* —Thanks, but I have my own connections." I then headed out to what the French used to call Rue Catinat, now named Tu Do Street. If you closed your eyes and reopened them, you could stand on Tu Do and think you were in a sleepy town in the southwest of France. A stone's throw from the Graham Green-ish Continental Hotel was Broddard's patisserie, probably the best bakery this side of Paris.

Next door was the Librairie de France, an immense bookstore that was a favorite browsing place for the French community—bored wives who had fled the plantations for a few days of shopping and perhaps a discreet assignation, elegant diplomats from Franco-phone countries who came in to buy Le Canard Enchainé and leaf through Paris Match. Further up the street towards John F. Kennedy Square and the Cathedral of Saigon was Le Pistou, a tiny bistro where I would meet my old friend, Yves Derrieu. Yves was eighty-five years old and used Le Pistou as his headquarters, sitting most of the day at a window-side table, watching the world go by.

His meanderings and recollections fascinated me. A lifelong resident of Saigon, he said he remembered when teeming Cholon, the Chinatown of Saigon, had been a *riziere*, a rice field. He patronized everybody and treated the locals with a dismissive kindness that was a trademark of the old colonial masters. According to him, the Americans were *cons*, fools, who didn't understand the Indochinese. When I asked him who *did* understand them, he shook his head full of white hair, rolled his eyes, and ordered another pastis.

Often, Yves and I just sat at his table and watched the world go by. I remember one scene that cracked us both up. An old Tonkinese crone was standing on the street with a rather flea-bitten parrot, apparently trying to sell the poor bird. Both the old woman and the parrot squawked unintelligibly to passersby without attracting much attention until a huge, black American soldier ambled up and began inspecting this avian wonder.

Both soldier and vendor began gesticulating wildly, engaging in what was an intense negotiation in languages that were mutually incomprehensible to both parties. Somehow the old woman managed to deliver a pitch line in English that consisted of the clincher, "Good bird, lotta words!" Impressed, the GI fished in his pocket and produced a fistful of *piastres,* which he shoved at the woman, who transferred the parrot from her arm to his. Far from speaking, the bird promptly screeched and bit his new owner on the nose, whereupon the GI fled and the parrot flew back to the old woman, who went cackling down the street into a back alley. To me, this scene summed up what was happening between the Americans and the Vietnamese in the trickery and mutual loss of respect that we had fallen into.

My favorite retreat was the CSS, Cercle Sportif Saigonais, an elegant urban country club set in the middle of the city that had been founded by the French in the nineteenth century. With its slow-moving ceiling fans, white-uniformed attendants gliding silently to and fro, and the whacking sounds of tennis balls intermingled with the tinkling laughter of its doomed upper-class members, the club had an *après moi le deluge* quality that fascinated and alarmed me. For those in the right place living in Saigon, it really was a lovely war.

It was at the club's poolside that I met Marie, a Eurasian doctoral student who was on holiday from Aix-en-Provence. She had come to Saigon to do some field research for her thesis about the penetration of Christian missionaries into Vietnam in the nineteenth century and to visit her aging father, who had been a minister in one of the earlier non-Communist governments. She introduced me to her parents, and I was surprised on a subsequent visit to their house when her mother presented me to some other guests as "*le fiancé de Marie.*"

Often at night we would go to her tiny apartment in a poor section of town. When I would leave in the early hours of the morning before dawn broke, I would walk for miles along the frangipani-fringed boulevards, inhaling the heady tropical smells of the blossoms and the sweet smell of incense smoke coming from the Buddhist temple on the road, knowing that I was contracting *le mal jaune,* yellow fever, that disease whose name the French had borrowed to denote Westerners who had become addicted to the mysterious East.

Her research completed, Marie went back to France, and I would follow her there after I left Vietnam. We would drive through the hills of Provence in the Renault I bought her and find little holes in the wall in Marseilles where we would eat Vietnamese food. Later, we said good-bye on a crowded subway in Paris when I told her I had to go my separate way and figure out who I was. A couple of years later when I was sorting out my life in Washington DC, I got a letter from her saying that she had married and that she was nauseated every day suffering from morning sickness.

Monsieur Yves had warned me about *metisses* or half-breeds, as he called French-Vietnamese Eurasians. He told me especially to stay away from Eurasian women since they had all of the faults of both races. But I found Marie to be just the opposite. I hope she is happy wherever she is.

When I returned to my hotel that night, I found the place crowded with people sitting on their suitcases in the lobby. I was told that the Communist forces had launched a coordinated, country-wide assault on the Americans and Vietnamese and that the country would surely fall within days. What came to be called the Tet Offensive signaled the beginning of the end for the American war in Vietnam even though the United States hung on for another seven years.

Some true believers said the Tet Offensive was a sure sign that we were winning and that the offensive was merely a last-gasp, frantic effort by the Communists to make a desperate, suicidal attempt before surrendering. That night, the atmosphere in Saigon was electric with fear and confusion. Somehow I ended up in a crowded discotheque thick with smoke and the sweet scent of marijuana. As the Ronnettes throbbed Motown rhythm, I found myself on the dance floor facing an undulating six-foot-two black woman, probably an embassy secretary. She shoved my nose into her breasts, and while we were doing our thing, I felt another pair of hands on my ass. It was hedonistic Saigon at its best. Later that night, I ran into an officer from the 1st Infantry Division who told me that An Loc had been destroyed during the Tet offensive. How many of my nine lives were left?

Hedonism was not limited to frantic crowds in packed dives trying to forget that a war was about to come crashing down on their heads. It was the signature lifestyle of our leader, the head of the U.S. pacification program, who was a civilian carrying the rank of general. He oversaw all of the nation-building programs in the largest region of the country, and held his subordinates to the highest standards of duty and service. But it was an open secret that he played by his own rules when it came to his personal life.

He habitually trolled English language academies and high schools in Saigon, chatting with young girls, many of them under age, charming them to meet him later in his luxurious villa, where he proceed to seduce them. These serial acts of statutory rape were ignored by the powers that be, just as the "collateral damage" that resulted in more than three million Indochinese deaths scarcely caused a ripple in the American media. After all, they were just gooks, weren't they? What was good for General Bull Moose and General Motors was good for America, even if this meant mass murder and the defiling of a country's young womanhood.

The more I contemplated the American presence in Indochina, the sicker I got. What had sucked us into this hideous undertaking and caused so many Americans, by and large decent people, to behave like savages? To say that we had not been warned would be to ignore the wise counsel of President Eisenhower in his farewell address when he cautioned the nation against the dangers of the military-industrial complex and how ruinous it could be for the country.

I thought back to my first year in Vietnam, when I had been a reports analyst working in Saigon and then Bien Hoa for this very same serial rapist. My job was to write reports that were favorable to the American effort, painting an optimistic picture without going over the top with Pollyannaish prevarication. I became skilled in the art of "nothing speak," honing my words into meaningless phrases, such as "It appears that significant progress has been made in recent months in certain areas of activity in a number of regions in the country, but much more needs to be done before our goals are fully realized." What was I doing writing such unadulterated crap when I knew that nothing was moving forward? Quite the contrary; in addition to the murderous saturation bombing of Vietnam, toxic chemicals of Agent Orange were being sprayed on the country's agriculture and rubber plantations so that the lifeblood of the economy and the health of the people were being ruined. Soon deformed babies would be born, the children of mothers who had worked the defoliated fields and rubber trees. We had a lot to be ashamed of.

One of my last acts before leaving Vietnam was to sit for the State Department's oral examination to become a career foreign service officer. Sometime earlier, I had passed the rather difficult written exam, which allowed me to proceed to the next step to becoming an American diplomat. One evening, I appeared before a stern panel of senior diplomats, who had assembled in the American Embassy in Saigon. The head of the panel was Phillip Habib, a gruff, Camel-smoking, but kindly man of ambassadorial rank, who grilled me relentlessly but fairly and announced at the end of the session that I had passed the test and had been accepted into the foreign service as a career officer.

He told me that there would be routine paper work and clearances to be carried out, but that in a matter of a few months, I would be on board. I shook hands with the august group, who congratulated me on my accomplishment. I was to learn in the coming months that their plaudits were premature. After I had returned to Washington DC, I was called into the State Department's personnel office in Foggy Bottom for what I assumed would be some routine signing of papers and the removal of the R from my FSO(R)-Foreign Service Officer (Reserve) designation.

I was mistaken. Instead I found myself facing a bureaucrat, an older woman, who without once looking me in the face, informed me that I had been terminated from the foreign service. Incredibly, when I asked her why, she replied that she did not know the reason. It was only later, years later and by sheer chance, that I was to find out that I had been terminated because a security investigation had come to the conclusion that I was gay. I had passed a rigorous test to get into a job that I had coveted since I was a child, and I had performed with honor and valor in the field in a dangerous war, Vietnam, and had been commended for it. Was this the recognition I deserved?

The coming months and years would give me much to think about, but as the old saying goes, "When the going gets tough, the tough get going." I would not be defeated by this unfortunate setback. Quite the contrary, it would set me on a clear personal path and a successful career that was to be far better than anything I could have realized had I been able to become an American diplomat. I would be less than honest if I were to say that I did not experience a slight rush of *Schadenfreude* seeing the frantic evacuation of the American Embassy in Saigon in 1975! Could I be blamed?

❧[CHAPTER SIX]❧

"CI VEDIAMO A LA BIRRERIA LAMA"*
A Year in Bologna, Italy

I stumbled upon the Birreria Lama by accident. I had just moved to Bologna and thought I would try a shortcut from my street, Via Oberdan, to the Piazza delle Due Torre and then on to Via Belmeloro, where I was studying at the Johns Hopkins campus next to the University of Bologna;

---

* Translation: "See you at the Lama Beer Hall."

the locals called our school l'Universita Americana. Following my rather uncertain sense of direction, I turned the corner on Via Oberdan and found myself in the tiniest of Vicolos, an alleyway, an ancient passage that must have been built in medieval times. Even on the brightest of days, Vicolo Mazzini was gloomy and dark because it had a "ceiling" that was actually the connection between the second story of two very old buildings up above, so that the sky was obscured. Ancient stonework surrounded me: I had the feeling of being in a cave or a grotto. It was the kind of space that one would avoid in New York City or Chicago, the perfect location for a mugging or even worse acts of violence.

As I exited the Vicolo into the blinding sunlight, I heard the din of voices and the clattering sound of flatware against plates. I found myself standing in front of what looked like a huge beer hall with a sign above double oak doors that said "Birreria Lama"; indeed, it was a beer hall, but as my twitching nostrils told me, it was also a restaurant. A medley of prosciutto, lasagna al forno, espresso, and other trademark Italian odors drew me inside, where I experienced the real Bologna. The scene before me could only be described as Brueghel-esque.

Both the noise level and the energy were jolting and energizing as I watched hundreds of working-class people dig into everyday dishes that would be considered specialties in the United States. As my eyes scanned the tables, I saw an incredible array of pastas, game, soups, salads, and desserts. Waiters were shouting orders to the galley, and customers, mostly men, were laughing and slapping each other on the back as they lifted glasses of Lambrusco, the deep purple-red wine of Emilia-Romagna. Through an opening in the wall behind the bar, I could glimpse the kitchen, where dozens of signoras labored over steamy cauldrons and sizzling pans, cackling and talking in the high-pitched, sing-song Bolognesi dialect that was generously peppered with old French words like "cinc franc"—instead of "cinque lire"—for "five lire."

My nose full of the smell of Bologna, I turned and left without eating, rushing to class, where I would have my first exposure to Italian politics. But it was in the Birreria Lama where I would really learn what was happening in Italy. I would spend a lot of time over the coming year in this rowdy, delicious stew-pot of a restaurant. It was where my grad school education would really take place.

Coming to Bologna had been a total accident. It was 1968; a few months earlier, I had arrived in Washington DC, fresh from the Tet Offensive in Vietnam, where the beginning of the end of America's involvement in a mistaken war was unfolding. Confused and on the verge of emotional collapse, I decided the most productive way to have a nervous breakdown was to go to graduate school and try to resolve my problems while studying. Perhaps burying myself in books would distract my troubled mind, I told myself, and in a couple of years I might emerge whole again and with another degree to peddle.

So I had applied to the Johns Hopkins School for Advanced International Studies (SAIS) in Washington DC, and had been accepted in the Master's Degree in International Relations program for the fall of 1968. My intent was to specialize in Asian studies, and although their catalogue advertised the existence of such a specialization, in reality it seemed that only a couple of courses on Asia were being offered. I shrugged off my initial disappointment at Hopkins being less than met the eye, at least in that particular field of study, and decided that perhaps I had had enough of Asia for a while. Two years in Vietnam during the height of hostilities had filled me with confusion and doubt about both the United States and myself.

I had saved a considerable sum of money while working in up-country Vietnam. The beauty of being in a war as far as personal finances were concerned was that there was no place to spend what one had earned. Housing was free, and food cost next to nothing if you fed yourself in the army mess hall or even if you chose to eat on the local economy; a bowl of phô, that delicious Vietnamese beef and noodle soup, cost all of ten cents back then. And there was really no place to go or anything to do that required money. Movies were free and beer dirt cheap at the compound canteen.

So I arrived in Washington DC flush with what seemed to be quite a lot of cash. But a fool and his money are quickly parted. Within two months, much of what I had earned and saved had been blown on ... exactly what, I'm not sure. But whatever it was, alcohol was involved. I had run into some army buddies from Vietnam and even one guy I had known when I was with the 64th Army Engineers in Libya, and we spent most of the summer of 1968 on bar stools in various dives in the nation's capital. I seem to recall that buying rounds of drinks for my friends would often include offering freebies to everybody else in the bar—the returning hero spreads his largesse type of thing. So by the time I reported to Johns Hopkins to register for classes, my finances were in shaky condition.

Normally the two-year master's degree program was spent at the Washington DC campus where most of the students were specializing in topics relating to the Atlantic alliance, Common Market issues, and the Cold War. I had no academic focus and just wanted to expose myself to some interesting courses taught by good professors. Any subject was okay. Still a creature of the military as far as rising early in the morning, I was the first student in line for registration when SAIS opened its doors at nine. I found myself facing Miriam De Grazia, the charming registrar, who reminded me of the glamorous film star Veronica Lake. Her hair fell over her face in the most charming way, and I wondered what a fetching creature like this was doing in such a boring job.

We chatted, and I told her I had just come back from Vietnam. I must have joked to her about being half-broke, because she suggested I go to SAIS Bologna for my first year. She said that Italy was dirt cheap and that I could live well over there on half the money I would spend in Washington. Although I had never heard of Bologna, I saw no reason to object to her suggestion and signed up to study there for my first year. After we had completed registration formalities, Miriam told me that Bologna was very much sought after and that I had been lucky to be there early and get one of the few openings that were available.

Later that day in the coffee shop, I overheard some of the other first-year students expressing their disappointment at not getting a Bologna slot. They were European specialists and had not gone to register till late morning. I laughed to myself and thanked the army for giving me the good habit of getting up early.

My classmates in Bologna were a varied bunch, coming mostly from the United States and Europe. There were a fair share of pampered heiresses whom I imagine never planned to actually work and who had come to SAIS to get a finishing school education that would equip them with brilliant cocktail conversation skills they would need later to navigate in the world of money and power from which they came. Then there were the very serious and rather brilliant Euro technocrats, mostly French, who had graduated from the *grandes ecoles* in Paris.

In their charming but slightly patronizing way, they were seeking exposure to the world beyond their rarified, elite environments and were attracted to the Americanness of SAIS Bologna. In the late sixties, the United States was still considered a cutting-edge country whose schools were to be emulated or attended if possible. I found the French the most interesting and at times slightly maddening with their ability to generate polemics and sustain an interesting argument with elegant, well-constructed reasoning that would often reach impossible conclusions that would, for example, support the French right to nuclear testing and alliances with third-world dictators of their choice while condemning the States for doing the same thing. No narrow mind is more dangerous than a highly educated one.

There were also a number of Italian students, and I ended up rooming with two of them. Gianfranco was from Trieste and was the son of a mid-level Italian diplomat. His goal was to follow in his father's footsteps and enter the Italian foreign service, which I was sure he would do, given the ease and fluency with which he spoke numerous languages. He was attractive and smooth and had a gorgeous, red-headed girlfriend with the unfortunate nickname of Pussy. In spite of his qualities and amiable nature, there was something mediocre about him, something clerical. Even then I could see him ending up in a menial position, perhaps a consular post, and never becoming an ambassador. I knew the charming Pussy had her sights set on the big brass ring and wished them luck.

Our other roommate was Sergio from Naples. Sergio was a nice fellow and the classic Italian *mammoni*, a mama's boy. From one of the great families of Naples, he received packages of goodies and phone calls from his mother almost every day. I seldom spoke with either of my roomies although the expressed purpose of their sharing digs with me was to improve their English. Gianfranco was seldom in the apartment except when Pussy visited from Rome, and then they were, understandably, indisposed to socialize. Sergio was the most intense and horrific cigarette smoker I had ever encountered. He seemed to chain-smoke from morning to night, and going in his room was to risk sudden asphyxiation.

My rapport with the other Bologna students was equally tenuous. Always a loner by nature unless cajoled into socializing, I went my separate way. Eating and people-watching in places like the Birreria Lama was more to my liking. It must have been in Lama that I met the person who was to become my best friend in Bologna. Walter was a *pelliciao*, a furrier, who designed and stitched mink coats that were the rage for both women and men in Italy during the sixties. Walter stood no more than five feet or five foot two at the most and rode a tiny child's bicycle when he traveled the streets of Bologna. I never found a diplomatic way of telling him how absolutely ridiculous he looked mounted on that little machine, so I kept my mouth shut.

Beady-eyed and possessed of a loud, booming voice far bigger than his pint size would have merited, Walter was not unattractive. He was compact and well-built and had a masculinity that most certainly attracted women. One of the most foul-mouthed people I have ever met, Walter taught me all of the Bolognesi dirty words he knew and was greatly amused to hear me curse him out in my American-accented Bolognese.

Sometimes Walter would spend the night at my place, and we would amuse ourselves late into the small hours, chatting about everything and nothing and engaging in childish games, like farting contests. I thought how funny life could be. The following morning, I would be in class with all of those French intellectuals and some world-class professor, discussing lofty topics like the global balance of power and the fate of the world, when just a few hours before, Walter and I had been engaged in a contest of flatulence. Were other people as weird as I was?

From time to time, we hung out with Carla, a six-foot-two Swedish-American girl who was also studying in Bologna and who, I think, had a crush on me. I always delighted in seeing Lilliputian Walter walking, arms linked in the Bolognesi manner, with the Amazonian Carla. They created quite a sight when we went for our *due passe* after-dinner strolls in the Piazza Maggiore.

Walter used to tell me about his life. He had an interesting past. He had been born in Asmara, Ethiopia—later to become Eritrea—when that country was an Italian colony. At some point, he and his parents had come back to Italy and had settled in the Emilia-Romagna region, a hot-bed of Communists and leftists. Walter was himself more prone to fascism and used to make pilgrimages to Predappio, a town a few miles away, where he would visit Dona Rachele, Mussolini's widow. She was very proud of the fact that she was drawing a pension as the widow of an Italian civil servant!

We would usually meet in the evening and have dinner together at Lama and then visit some of his Italian friends. I remember once after eating, we went for a ride with two of his girlfriends in their new Fiat. We passed a seminary with lots of nuns and priests at the entrance, and the girls threw them the finger and yelled, "*Vaffanculo!*"; some of the priests threw the finger right back at us. Italy may have been the seat of Roman Catholicism, but the country was suffused with an earthy secularism that even extended to its clergy.

Another couple I met through Walter were Communists. At that time, Emilia-Romagna and Bologna were run by a Communist government, and Bologna was the seat of the PCI, the Italian Communist Party. I went to a number of PCI meetings and rallies with Anna and Federico, and I came to realize before long that Italian Communism was more akin to FDR New Dealism than anything resembling what was coming out of Moscow. We would visit Anna's father, who was a professor at the University of Bologna and a member of the PCI central committee.

He was a gentle man and would tell us stories of his role in the resistance fighting the fascists. Later when he finished his lectures, we would listen to scratchy old records on his gramophone with Giovanna Daffini belting out socialist anthems and singing songs of the downtrodden rizzaio, the women workers in the rice fields of northern Italy who became famous in leftist Italy as symbols of working-class revolutionary fervor.

Due to my impecunious bar-hopping while I was chilling out in Washington DC, I found myself on the verge of being broke when I arrived in Bologna. I had my meager veteran's educational benefits in the form of a monthly stipend, as well as a small grant from SAIS Bologna. I started giving English lessons to a number of well-heeled Italians, including the owner of a factory. He was an Italian count named Conte Guido Sosoli de Bianci. And luckily, I discovered a source of good, cheap food. Buried in a cavelike cavity in a medieval building near the university was a shop that only sold bruised fruit, produce that was a bit old and slightly smashed and not very good-looking on a shelf. Still, it was delicious and sold for next to nothing. I called the place the Used Fruit Store, and it kept me going for the rest of the academic year. Most of the other customers were people who were a bit down on their luck. I was glad to be in the socialist paradise of Bologna!

Through my contacts in Bologna, thanks to Walter and the Birreria Lama, I found out more about what was really happening in Italian politics than I would have learned in SAIS Washington DC, where the professors were in the thrall of Cold Warrior thinking. I was coming to what I felt was an interesting realization. It seemed to me that Italian thinking, indeed European thinking, was much more nuanced than the American way of looking at the world, which was more simplistic, more black and white—more "I'm okay, you're not okay."

Probably such a simple-minded perspective of the world came from the immense power that America had come to possess. I wished that it were otherwise. Then tragedies like the Vietnam War could have been avoided. One evening at Lama, when we had had more than our share of fizzy Lambrusco wine with our lasagna, Walter announced that he had figured out Americans. He told me he had been reading seriously about the United States and had learned that Americans were addicted to canned food and circuses. I thought about what he had said and came to the conclusion that he was correct. Today that analysis could be revised to read fast food and trashy TV.

Bologna was the seat of the oldest university in Europe and one of the most beautiful and logically constructed cities I had known. With miles and miles of elegant *gallerie* or covered walkways, one could walk for miles and miles in the historic center on a rainy day without getting wet. In the center of town were the Due Torre, the two towers, that Dante said used to move when you bent back and looked at their peaks with the rushing clouds streaking by above them.

Near the two towers was a senior home for retired opera singers. I used to go there sometimes on rainy afternoons for a coffee and a chat with its inhabitants, who were eager to reminisce and at times burst into song if the right hints were dropped. The Bolognesi were sophisticated and worldly in their own way, as members of an ancient culture are wont to be, but when it came to food, they drew the line. Anything not Italian was considered exotic or downright strange.

I remember when some misguided soul opened a Chinese restaurant on my street. The façade of the restaurant was a glass window looking into the kitchen, where Asian chefs were cooking with their woks. Big crowds used to gather in front of the window and watch the chefs at work, but inside, the restaurant was almost totally empty except for a few American medical students eating chop suey. Once as I stood with the spectators gawking at the cooking show, I could not resist asking one couple if they had tried the food. Laughing, they replied that they would *never* dream of eating Chinese food; they just liked to watch the chefs in action.

In those days, Bologna was a city of bicycles, and I became an avid cyclist, pedaling to and from school almost every day, even in the rain, when I held an open umbrella with one hand while steering through the crowded streets with the other. Sometimes I would pass my friend and classmate, Olga, walking to school, and she would hop on the back of my bike and ride along with me.

As a Communist-administered city, Bologna was efficient and clean and offered such perks as free city bus rides to its inhabitants. This municipal excellence did not extend to the post office, however. I remember sending out over one hundred Christmas cards in December 1968, and sad to say, not one of my friends received their card. I am heartened to know that the postal services have improved.

In September 2009, at the request of an American friend living in Todi, I mailed him a jar of Vaseline. Several weeks later, he told me that the Italian police had contacted him about a certain package that had arrived in Italy with his name on it. It appeared that the Vaseline was suspicious to them and had the appearance of being a container full of explosive material. It was good to know that Italy had not only become vigilant in regard to terrorists; the postal service seemed to be working, too.

With Italy's excellent train service, I was able to travel easily and cheaply to many places. I was especially fond of taking the Milano-Rome express, called the Sette Bello— the Seven-Card Stud. It was a luxury train that served gourmet food as we streaked through the countryside at more than a hundred miles per hour, which was fast in those days. I would get on the train in the late morning in Bologna and arrive in Rome before dinner. I usually stayed with my friend Carlo, who was from Umbria.

Once he invited me home with him to visit his parents in Perugia, and they told me how, as a baby, the little blonde

Carlo was the darling of the Nazi Germans when they occupied the town. They would throw him in the air and catch him, calling him Piccolo Tedesco. Carlo lived in a tiny apartment in an ancient building, and his next-door neighbors were old ladies who were seamstresses for the cardinals in the Vatican. They stitched all of their Eminences' garments and were loving, rosary-clutching, gossipy ladies. Once on a visit to Rome, I fell ill with flu, and they mothered me with the Italian version of a Jewish mother's chicken soup.

By now I had fallen in love with the Italian language, as beautiful and useless as it was. Sometimes I found myself thinking, *Why aren't I learning another language like Spanish, which could be used in so many countries around the world? Where can you travel outside Italy and use Italian?* Maybe in Ethiopia or Libya, if you ran into some older person who had been around before 1945, when those places were Italian colonies, but otherwise it had limited utility. Still, I thrilled when I heard beautiful Florentine-accented Italian spoken.

I loved to sit in the Bologna train station and just listen to the announcements over the loudspeaker in those exquisitely accented tones: "*In arrivo al binario quattro il Settebello da Firenze.*" What was it about Italian that was so beautiful? I think I found the answer when I learned to sing some opera arias in both Italian and English. The words seemed to roll off my tongue when it was in Italian. In English, it was another story. Somehow, when I sang, it just sounded utilitarian. Not at all beautiful.

Another friend in Rome I sometimes stayed with was Ernesto. Ernesto worked for the Christian Democratic Party as a political trouble-shooter. He used to travel the globe, connecting with other Christian Democratic parties, mostly in Europe and Latin America. I came to realize through knowing Ernesto and his friends the strong connection between politics and the Catholic Church. I suspected the hand of the CIA was also involved in many of his maneuvers when he was dispatched to "fix" something somewhere.

I had become a total devotee of Italian food and somewhat of a fanatic in the pursuit of excellent dishes. I once traveled hours to the rather grubby port town of Piombino to sample what was reputed to be the country's finest *spaghetti alle vongole*—spaghetti with clams. It was worth the trip! From Bolognesi friends, I also learned the characteristics of various Italian cities. The Venetians were all reputed to be crazy; it was that fog from the canals that went to their brains. The Bolognesi were sexy, and the Genovese were the stingiest.

The joke was that a bunch of Genovese were trapped in an avalanche in a hut in the Italian Alps. When the Red Cross came to rescue them and knocked on the door, saying, "It's the Red Cross!" the Genovese replied, "Don't bother us; we already donated!" Of course, the Bolognesi reserved for themselves the reputation of being the sexiest city, *Bologna la Grassa*. It was an historical fact, Walter told me, that Bologna invented fellatio.

In the sixties, most everybody in Bologna wore tailor-made clothes. I found an excellent tailor in Via Zamboni and had a full wardrobe of suits made along with a handsome coat. The Italian style at that time was to cut men's clothing so it was very tight-fitting. Bright colors were also very much in fashion.

When I returned to Washington DC some months later, I lifted quite a few eyebrows wearing my gigolo-tight suits and yellow socks. I'm glad I didn't run into any of my old army buddies when I was suited up in my Continental rags. I still keep one Via Zamboni suit in my closet to remind me of Bologna and how thin I used to be!

Although I thought of Bologna often after I left, I never managed to go back until a few years ago, when I traveled up from Rome for nostalgic visit. I would be seeing Bologna again after almost forty years! My main objective, of course, was to go back to the Birreria Lama. I hoped I would see Walter there and we could eat and drink like truck drivers and insult each other in gutter Bolognese and catch up on the decades that had passed so quickly. What would he look like? Would he recognize me? Had he married? How was his business? Did he have children? Could I see his wife's picture?

I alighted from the train and took a bus into the center of town and held my breath as I got near the Due Torre. Memories came rushing back as I stood for a moment beneath the ancient towers. I stretched so I could see the sky and the racing clouds and experience the illusion of the towers moving. I then made a beeline for Vicolo Mazzini and Lama, but it was not there. In its place was a fast food restaurant and a bunch of skate boarders hanging out where Walter and I used to stand and chat.

My heart sank, and I hoped for a minute that somehow I had come to the wrong place or that Lama had just moved to another location. Surely it had? Then I asked a passerby what had happened to La Birreria Lama, and shaking his head, he said that it had closed a few months earlier. I felt completely lost and crushed with disappointment. I walked the city's streets for hours. None of the old mom-and-pop trattorie had survived. Everything was Burger King and KFC. Where was the Italian food? What did Italians eat these days?

Then I went to my old street, Via Oberdan, to see my friend Renaldo, the handsome young man who ran a dry goods store. When I got to his shop, I saw a Pakistani face looking out at me from behind the cash register. Most of the small shops in Bologna had been taken over by South Asians. Globalization had arrived in Bologna with a bang. My only consolation was to walk to Piazza Maggiore, where we had spent so many evenings engaged in that most civilized of Italian rituals, the after-dinner stroll. As I stood silently looking at the elegant church at the center of the piazza, I thought I heard Walter laughing behind me. I turned with a smile, hoping to see my old friend, but there were only two happy Italian students enjoying the evening. Walter and I had been like that forty years earlier.

❧[CHAPTER SEVEN]❧

I LOVE PARIS
Being Young and Poor in Lutece

When I lived in Paris in the late sixties, I fell in with what the French called *les biches*, the bright young things, a decidedly upper-class type of French person, those people whom today one might refer to as the BCBG crowd, the *bon chic bon gens*, beautiful people. I nicknamed them the *de people* because most of them had the noble handle *de* before their names. There was Sophie de Montgolfier, whose great grand-something had invented the Montgolfier, the first lighter-than-air balloon. Audouin de l'Epine was blonde, six foot three, with a chiseled face and from a noble family.

With Audouin, who was one of the nicest people I ever met, everything was "simple, tres simple"; as in: our estate in the Camargue has a pool and a tennis court but everything is very simple. Then there was Damien Pasquier-Desvignes, whose family had been making wine since 1428. He invited me to the family seat in Burgundy, and every afternoon when we finished our game of tennis, we would roam the chateau's wine cellar to find the right liquid accompaniment for dinner. The wines we chose had no commercial labels on them, just hand-written or simply typed nomenclatures like "Saint Lager 1938" or "Bourgogne 1946." Pierre de Faucigny-Lucinge was very British and spoke French with an English accent, pronouncing "Megeve" as "Magave"; that was where the family had a ski lodge, but he assured me that actually everything up in that jet-set spa was really very simple. It seemed to me that wealth and power in France was simplicity incarnate.

I'm not sure exactly how it was that I came to hang out with this rarified group of beautiful people. It may have been through my friend and classmate, Florence, who was a charter member of the French haute bourgeoisie. We had gone to school together in Bologna, Italy, and both of us ended up being in Paris in 1969 and started doing things together, which naturally led to my meeting some of her French friends and then friends of those friends. So in a matter of a few months, I had a large number of French acquaintances, some of whom became lifelong connections.

The whole process of getting to know these people was an education to me and showed me that France, in addition to possessing the usual upper, middle, and lower class distinctions found in most countries, also had a divide that I will call north-south. It was a divide that was best understood by looking at a map of France. At the risk of oversimplification—and nothing is ever simple in France in spite of Audouin's assurances to the contrary—drawing a line through the country from west to east so that it passed well below Limoges and Clermont-Ferrand, grim Clermont-Ferrand as *les biches* would say, rolling their eyes at just the mention of that unfortunate factory town, you would end up with two Frances, the northern Anglo one and the southern Mediterranean zone.

The two were as different as night and day, and it was this contrasting—indeed, conflicting—mixture that made France such a fascinating place. To be sure, other countries, Italy and Spain, had similar divides; somebody from Milan had little in common with a *paisan* from Sicily, but in France it seemed to me to be more pronounced. The Anglos, as the name implies, tended to be more "English," their manner of speaking and comportment tended to be spare, crisp, and minimal—no flailing about of arms and hands when discussing a bouillabaisse recipe or talking about a train being late. There was less outward display of emotion: the cool versus the passionate.

The two worlds often collided. I remember boarding an Air France plane from Paris to Nice where a fist fight broke out over who had the last seat. More passengers kept boarding the flight until the aisles were full of travelers standing packed against each other, not unlike the Lexington Avenue number 6 train at rush hour! A clash between the French north and the French south. The BCBG, Anglo-inclined crowd thought such a ruckus unacceptable; the Meds would say that people have to stand up for their rights.

I was never sure why *les biches* liked me. I was nothing out of the ordinary and had no particular talents or entertaining characteristics, nor was I particularly handsome or rich; in fact, I was poor at that time. I think it was simply because I was American and it was, perhaps, de rigueur at that moment in time in France to have an American around. I began to feel like a court jester or a performing seal.

I knew my friends thought it was always fun to hear French spoken with an American accent. That made me exert great effort to speak correct "French French." I think it is deeply carved in human nature to want to be accepted by one's peers on an equal basis and sort of fade into the woodwork, even at the expense of losing the attention-getting notoriety that in the beginning may be a titillating sensation but which sets us apart and makes us feel like strangers. In any case, I made many friends during my year in France, and still to this day, forty years later, stay in touch with a number of them. The French are not as quick to glad hand and first-name as Americans are wont to do, but once you have them as your friend, it is forever and always.

I also learned from my beautiful people the incredible importance to the French of having the "right" education, of going to *les grandes ecoles*, the great schools. Career tracks are built around graduating from ENA (National Administration School), Science Po (the faculty of political science), HEC (the leading French business school), and several other institutions. One simply does not succeed in the worlds of power and wealth without education from these hallowed places.

Perhaps because it is France, this is not a bad thing. Until the fifties, French politics were characterized by frequently changing governments. It was not uncommon for a prime minister to be voted out in a matter of months. What held the country together for generations during these unstable times was the highly centralized French civil service and the superbly trained, top-level technocrats who had been schooled at *les grandes ecoles*.

Two personal experiences illustrate how well-organized and responsive the French government can be to the smallest problems of people who are not even French citizens. Once on a skiing trip, I was accosted by a French customs officer at the French-Swiss border and asked to produce a bill of sale for the skis I was carrying, which appeared to him to be new. I had no such receipt and was heavily fined for my alleged oversight. Another time, I was dragged off the Metro by subway attendants when I had mistakenly entered the first-class car and only had a second-class ticket to show them. Again I received a stiff fine. In both cases, I wrote to the French government, in the latter instance to the RATP, the subway system, and for the earlier problem to the Ministry of Finance. Within a couple of weeks, I received a personally written communication, not a form letter, along with a check apologizing for the actions of the officials concerned. I am certain that had these encounters occurred in the United States, the treatment and the result would have been less satisfactory. I am therefore a great fan of the French system and the way it operates, especially the French civil service.

I am getting ahead of myself. Let's go back to the first time I visited France, which was in the fall of 1963. I was a soldier in the American army, assigned to a huge military base in Tripoli in what was then the Kingdom of Libya. Mohammed Khadafi was an obscure lieutenant at the time. One of the perks of military life in those days was the ability to hitchhike rides on MATS (Military Air Transport System) aircraft to almost anywhere in the world, provided one had leave time accumulated. I used my leave to hitch rides to a number of places in Europe, Edinburgh, Naples and Paris being the three I best remember.

It is hard to describe the thrill of being in Paris as a young person for the first time. I arrived in October of 1963 when I was twenty-four. I had read the glorious history of France and had studied French in school, and now I was actually there. I spent my short couple of days wandering the streets and boulevards, frequenting lots of cafes, standing at *le zinc*, the counter in bars, watching the world go by. My favorite place was La Brasserie Alsacienne, an atmospheric place at the tip of the Ile Saint Louis where it joins the small foot bridge connecting it to the larger Ile de La Cite, the two main islands in the River Seine.

Over the years I would come back again and again to the Ile, which became my favorite place in Paris. I made friends with a young, blonde Alsatian named Gino who was a waiter at La Brasserie. Thirty-five years later when I returned to Paris for a visit, Gino was still there at the restaurant, but he had moved from waiting tables to being the manager and was now wearing a jacket and tie. That's another thing I like about France: there is continuity.

I put up in a little hotel in the Latin Quarter in rue Serpente called Hotel Littre. Back then, even a GI on a tiny salary could afford a nice little bohemian accommodation in Paris. The first morning there was an immense downpour. Over and over again, I drilled myself in my room, practicing the French I planned to use when I descended to the lobby. Since the weather demanded it, I would say, "*Il fait beau temps pour les canards!*—Lovely weather for ducks." I opened the elevator door, entered the lobby, and announced to the only person there, the *Gaulois*- puffing concierge, that it was indeed lovely weather for ducks. She looked up, cigarette hanging from her lip, and continued mopping the floor, saying nothing.

I thought she must not have heard me, so I repeated my little weather-related sentence about the ducks. Once again, she looked up with what I could describe as a semijaundiced glare, and with a Gallic shrug, grunted, *"Ah, mais oui! C'est normal!"* My first exchange with the French race had been consummated. Basic lesson in France: never interrupt a concierge when she is doing something, even if it is reporting you to the Gestapo. Concierges are uncrowned royalty in France. You wait for *them* to recognize you.

I was glad I got to Paris in 1963. Back then, you could still see the old France as it had been for centuries. In just a few years, things began changing very rapidly, some for the good, some not so good. Then the phones barely managed to function; now they are superb. Then there were pissoirs along the main roads where men could stop to relieve themselves. These rather unseemly but convenient facilities were gone by the seventies. Their disappearance was one of many steps to sanitize Paris, another being the sand-blasting of the Cathedral de Notre Dame. Somehow seeing this great monument glistening white robs it of its history. Better leave some things alone, I say.

The belly of Paris, the central market of Les Halles, which had been feeding the population since the Middle Ages, was still very much alive and well when I first visited the city. Smack in the middle of the busiest section of town, it was a nightmare of traffic jams and noisy altercation, but it was so atmospheric. It is said that George Gershwin got some of his inspiration for "American in Paris" from the honking and shouting that was the music of this vital, totally Gallic place.

One night, I stayed up till dawn walking the streets and ended up at Les Halles at four in the morning. Things were just getting underway at that hour, and the famous all-night joints of Le Chat Qui Peche and Le Chien Qui Fume were catering to tuxedoed gents and ladies in evening gowns side by side with stevedores and truck drivers. Not long after I was there, the market moved out of the city to Rungis on the road to the airport. Paris has never been the same since.

Another thing I loved were the old city buses. Most of them were ancient machines that had been put in service around the time of First World War and, incredibly, were still carrying passengers forty years later. The best way to ride in them was to stand at the back where there was a little balcony, like the end of the old railroad cars where presidential candidates would stand to deliver stump speeches.

Sitting at sidewalk cafés could be an interesting experience. I found that I was often chatted up by women of a certain age. One afternoon on the Champs Elysees, one of them approached me and said she had been a teenager in 1945 when the Americans liberated Paris. She confided that she had had a GI boyfriend and that Americans were very nice. I bought her a drink and then departed, wishing her good luck—good luck at what, I was not sure.

My next visit to Paris was in 1965, when I was passing through on my way from Switzerland to the United States and then, as it turned out, to Vietnam. I had hitchhiked with my enormous backpack and got a ride non-stop from Lausanne to Paris. My host on the road trip dropped me off right in the middle of Les Halles! It was the fourteenth of July, Bastille Day, France's commemoration of its liberation from tyrannical monarchy, and later that evening, I found myself once again on the Ile-Saint Louis, reveling with other young celebrants.

That was where I met Isabelle. Along with her other friends, we celebrated throughout the night and, with a serious hangover, I went straight to the airport without a wink of sleep that same morning and flew to Washington DC. We stayed in touch, and I wrote her from Vietnam. Some months later I got a non-invitation wedding announcement. The card said that Isabelle and Roland had been married in a small ceremony that included only family.

I found that an interesting way to deal with a wedding. I wrote her back wishing her the best. She had become a doctor, and several years later when I had returned to Paris to live and work, I ran into her on the street just outside of my office. We chatted for a few seconds and then said good-bye, two lives that had intersected in their youth and then moved on. As I walked back to my office, I reflected on what might have been and if Isabelle had ever thought I wanted to marry her.

I had had many inconclusive encounters with women, and I was starting to think that maybe I was leading them on when almost always that was not my intention. It is nicer today being old—I am seventy now—when the pressure to get hitched is no longer in the air.

My exit from Vietnam in the spring of 1968 was a strange time for me. I was reeling from the experience of fighting for two years in a mistaken war that could never have been won, combined with a professional setback, having been being terminated from my State Department job because of a homosexual experience I had had in college. The snoops found that out when they did a background investigation on me.

I returned to the United States and Washington DC on the day that Martin Luther King was assassinated and found the nation's capital to be at war with itself. There was a curfew, the sound of gunshots in the air, whole blocks of the city on fire, and military helicopters flying overhead. I thought I was coming home to a peaceful country but I had stepped into another war.

Then I left the States for France in May, just in time for the revolution of May 1968, when Paris and the rest of the country were practically closed down. I had come back to France because I loved it and also to meet Marie, the Eurasian woman I had known in Vietnam who was my fiancée. At this point in my life, I felt pretty sure that I would never marry a woman, and I had to break this news to her in the best way possible.

We met and talked, and I told her how I felt. We decided to part ways, and I asked her what she wanted to do with *nounours*, the childhood teddy bear that was her most prized possession. She had given it to me back in Saigon when we were together, and I had carried it with me everywhere I went. We had joked that it was our first child. She said I should keep it. We were on the Metro, the Paris subway, when we saw each other for the last time and parted. We smiled at each other and said good-bye as I exited the train. I stood on the platform holding *nounours* and waving farewell as the doors closed and the train moved on.

I roamed Paris for several days—more accurately, several nights. I was staying in a flop house of a hotel on Ile Saint-Louis, which today has become a five-hundred-dollar-a-night boutique inn. My routine was to sleep until noon, have a couple of stiff coffees and a baguette, and then set out and walk the city. I would climb the steps of Montmartre up to Sacre Coeur Cathedral. From there, the panorama of Paris was spectacular, a bird's-eye view. Off in the distance was the Eiffel Tower. I realized that in all of my time in the City of Lights that I had never been up this famous monument. It remains a project I will fulfill one of these days.

During my nocturnal amblings, I almost got killed or at least seriously bludgeoned. The May '68 Revolution had reached a fevered pitch, with strikes and student demonstrations throughout the city. Revolutionary poster art abounded. "It is Forbidden to Forbid" was the theme. Then the police started to get tough, and the big question mark in the equation, the Communist Party and the labor unions, made their move to support the government and the police against the students. It was a big surprise to everybody.

Law enforcement became relentless and the feared CRS, the French special police, were called out. One night I emerged from a bar rather well-oiled and decided to walk down a narrow alley. Whistling to myself and weaving along the cobblestones, I was suddenly faced with hundreds of desperate student strikers running for their lives towards me with the helmeted CRS in hot pursuit. What should I do?

To quote Jean-Paul Sartre, there was no exit. I joined the crowd of fleeing students, running involuntarily as their point man. Then in front of me I saw another phalanx of CRS planted in our path. I would surely be pummeled to pieces by these brutes if I didn't extricate myself from this stampede. Thank God for obscure little doorways in crumbling old Paris buildings. I ducked into one just in time and let the thundering herd of students rush to their tormentors. The next day in the papers I read about the blood and injuries to the crowd I had been leading!

"Attention, Sam! Vous etes dans le courant d'air!—Be careful, Sam, you are standing in a draft of air!" As she blurted out these words, tiny Paulette body-blocked me, shoving me out of the drafty doorway of her office at the Atlantic

Institute, which was an airy, old place. It was 1969, and I had returned to Paris once again, this time not as a traveler passing through but as a resident who had a job. The French were famously alert to the danger of *courants d'air*, air currents or drafts, and petite Paulette was only doing her duty as a good French person to take me out of harm's way.

To this day, I thank her for instilling in me the valuable knowledge about treacherous air currents, so damaging to the liver and other vital humors. I have become a firm believer—the converted are always the most fervent—and I often get into serious altercations with Americans at my gym in New York when they turn on fans in the exercise rooms. "I only have one liver!" I tell them. The Americans are opposite to the French in many ways; probably the most basic difference is about air currents. If this issue could be resolved, I am sure that all Franco-American enmity would disappear overnight.

I had just completed a year of graduate school in Bologna, Italy, at the Johns Hopkins University campus abroad, and I was supposed to go back to Washington DC for the second and final year of a master's program. I learned about a gap-year job that was being offered by the Atlantic Institute in Paris. It was a small boutique research organization that examined questions relating to the Atlantic Alliance between Europe and the United States and other issues involving the future of what was then called the Common Market, now known as the European Union. They were looking for a research assistant and general factotum. I interviewed successfully for the job, and even though it meant putting off the completion of my studies, it gave me what I had longed to have: the experience of living in France and seeing life unfold there on a day-to-day basis. I had become a total Francophile, and the prospect of "becoming French" was exciting to me. I wondered if I would I end up loving them more or less after my year there.

The Atlantic Institute was located in the middle of the 16th Arrondisement, considered to be the most bourgeois neighborhood in the city. Everybody had Spanish maids who herded well-groomed children of French CEOs to their exclusive schools. Ladies took three-hour lunches in the neighborhood's Michelin-starred restaurants. It was the Upper East Side of Paris. I ended up living in this posh *quartier*, but in the lower section, the bowels of it, along Avenue de Versailles, not far from the Citroen automobile factory in Boulogne-Billancourt.

When talking to *les biches*, I was always careful to be vague about just where I lived in the 16th. If they had known it was near Billancourt, I'm sure I would have become toast with the little darlings. I found a studio apartment, and even though it was Spartan because this was France, it had a proper bidet in the bathroom. I used the bidet to soak my dirty underwear. The flat was on the ground floor, far to the back of the building. Walking through the lobby was not convenient and always involved dealing with the concierge, who was a real Madame de Farge; she seemed to always have something to complain about. To avoid her, I used to leave my living room window open and enter my apartment by going around the building and just stepping through the window into the flat. It was just like what I thought Jacques Tati might do if he lived in my place.

Working at the Atlantic Institute was fun, although I don't think I ever succeeded in explaining to my mother or my grandmother just what I was doing there. My mother persisted in thinking that I was involved in something to do with oceanography, and because of her defective hearing, Grandma believed I was selling antiques when I told her I was employed at a place with the name "Atlantic." To her it sounded like "antique."

It was an operation funded almost exclusively by the Ford Foundation and provided a pasture for retired American ambassadors to wile away their time after they had left the U.S. foreign service. The director of the institute was always a retired American diplomat. Its activities consisted mostly in organizing and hosting seminars and workshops and commissioning well-known thinkers, like Pierre Uri and Henri Aron, to write papers on important world issues.

For our meetings, we would select pleasant spots, such as Cascais, Portugal, where we would go for a weekend by the sea, having hired gurus to examine the state of the world and listen to these geniuses from Harvard and Oxford make pronouncements about the "panglossian" state of things. I really came to hate that expression "panglossian" and all of the slick, self-satisfied, potted nonsense that came with it. Leave it to me to become dissatisfied with even the best of situations. I came to loggerheads with the director when he confronted me over my choice of David Halberstam, the well-known writer, as a lead participant in one of our meetings. He backed me against the wall, accusing me of being dim-witted in selecting somebody who had been critical of the Ford Foundation. Heaven forbid! Damn the truth and freedom of expression! Biting the hand that fed one and bankrolled a chauffeur-driven Citroen and fat-cat apartment was a no-no, even though I had managed to bag a Pulitzer-Prize-winning author. I was glad my year at the Atlantic Institute was coming to an end. This was not my first run-in with the dimwits who run American foreign policy.

Looking back on my days in Paris, I can't believe how much I did and how many experiences I had. My French had become fluent and colloquial, and I was meeting all sorts of people, not just beautiful ones. One friend, Francois, was from Normandy and was really simple in the good sense, not like Audouin's swimming pool was simple. He invited me for the weekend to his family's place in Caen, saying a very special and "delicious" event had been planned that I would certainly enjoy.

We drove through the beautiful French countryside, arriving at the family farm in late afternoon, just in time to get ready for dinner. I then learned what the special event was. It was about tripes, the specialty of Normandy. Francois's father was famous for cooking this dish, and his tripes had been selected as an entry at the International Tripe Competition to be held in Montreal. The tripes would be cooked and flown to their destination, where they would be judged by an international tribunal of tripes experts.

Francois said we would be having this wonderful dish that night for dinner; his father had cooked what was kind of a dress rehearsal to the main event some days away. I hated tripes, truly hated them. It was one of the few dishes in the world I could not bear. All of those intestines, the squishy masses and tubes floating around in a bilious gravy. I almost fainted when he told me what we were eating that night. I have mostly blocked that evening from my memory and can only recall getting very drunk. I have no recollection whatsoever of the food I consumed. And I never heard how the tripes did in Montreal.

Much of Parisian life is lived on the streets and in the cafes along the boulevards. I loved frequenting one café on the Boulevard Saint-Germain and used to wile away hours with a coffee or a wine in my hand. When the weather got a bit cold, the cafes served *vin chaud*, hot spicey wine. One afternoon, I was with an English friend from the office. She was a delightful, lovely, intelligent woman, and we often did things together. The only thing with Millicent was mornings. She was a total dragon in the morning, and everybody at the office avoided her like the plague until lunchtime. Luckily it was 4:00 p.m., and the shadows were already getting long, and Millicent was in good spirits.

We were indulging in hot wine and chatting when I looked up and saw a thin young man walking on a wire he had strung up between lampposts on the street by the café. His balance was amazing, and he topped off his act by standing on one foot for the longest time. After he descended and passed his hat for coins, we asked him to join us for a drink. He was Philippe Petit. He must have been about nineteen or twenty years old at the time. He told us he had come from a Russian family of circus performers and that he was following in the tradition of his father, who had also started out as a street performer.

After that day, I used to see Philippe around Paris, and he kept in touch for while and would invite me to special performances. His wire-walking got more daring and beautiful every time he did it. A few years later, I was amazed to pick up the *New York Times* and see my friend Philippe in a photograph that showed him walking on a wire stretched between the two towers of the World Trade Center in Manhattan. I think that was in the early seventies. Last year, 2008, a film was made of his daring adventure, called *Man on Wire*. I still remember him that cold November day in Paris when he was just starting out, collecting coins from people on the street. Paris was a magical place.

Somehow I managed to keep up with everything that was happening in Paris. I went to La Comédie Francaise for Moliere, whom I loved. The French stage was excellent in those years, with actresses such as Suzanne Flon and Madeleine Renault appearing in dramas and comedies. I was a great fan of French satirical comedy cabaret and followed some of the troupes avidly. I also managed to get into various productions that were sold out.

In August, there was a lot of buzz about an American production that was going to be held in a tent in the space where the old Les Halles market had been. It was experimental and was said to be mostly in the nude. France was no stranger to nudity, but somehow the fact that the nudes were Americans seemed to excite the French imagination. I went down to see what it was all about. When I got there, it was mayhem with limousines lined up and all manner of famous people queuing.

I walked up to the head of the line and watched a policeman turn away Anthony Quinn and Juliette Greco. They wheedled and cajoled to no avail. She smiled at the policeman, and Anthony Quinn offered his autograph. Still no luck. When a French *flic* says, "Non!" he means "Non!" On impulse, I went over and ducked under the tent and entered the enclosure. When the policeman stopped me, I nonchalantly looked at him and said, matter-of-factly, "Je suis figurant—I'm an extra." He said, "Allez-y," and waved me through. Eat your heart out, Anthony and Juliet. Being young and adventuresome in Paris had its thrills!

That year in Paris was a beautiful period in my life, and I will always treasure the memories and the friends I made. It was also a sad time. I had entered an unfortunate netherworld of confusion, not knowing if I was gay or straight. Well, not exactly. I knew I was interested in men but I was afraid to recognize and act upon my emotions. I continued seeing women, and the relationships invariably ended when they saw I was not really involved. It would take me a few more years to resolve these deep-seated issues and emerge a happy, balanced person. I like to think that Paris helped me make the right decision.

[CHAPTER EIGHT]

CHAO PHRAYA SERENADE
Memories of Living in Thailand

My old house in Bangkok sits near the water's edge at the Theves boat dock. Romanized Thai words are very misleading when it comes to pronouncing them correctly. In the case of Theves, it is pronounced "Tay Wait." But to get the pronunciation really correct you have to say those two words with falling tones. That's sort of hard to explain in writing, but for lack of a better explanation, try pronouncing them as though you were gently exasperated—as though you were asking a lover to repeat something he said because the first time he had mumbled the words and they were unintelligible to you. Think irritated but infatuated, and that will get it. In Thailand, always act as though you were infatuated and you will never go wrong.

I'm glad that when I first came to Thailand I took the linguistic plunge most foreigners avoid, thinking that Thai is such a difficult language it could never possibly be mastered by a *farang*. It's just not true. In a matter of weeks, I learned the writing system, which only has thirty-some letters; suddenly signs and posters on the street came alive with meaning. It was like being blind and then gaining my sight back, although a friend joked about the questionable utility of learning to read Thai. "You see a shop with medicine on the shelves. You don't have to read the Thai sign outside to know it's a pharmacy!" Whatever.

My writing out a simple sentence in Thai was a source of unending amusement to the locals, who would laugh when they saw me painstakingly scribble a few words in a childlike scrawl. I took language classes at a school called AUA, and my teacher, Khun Mattana, was a kindly tyrant who operated by the drill method, urging us to repeat and repeat. At the end of the six-week class, she called me over to her desk. I thought she was going to tell me something about how I had been a good student, but instead she complimented me on the way I walked.

She said that most *farang* (foreign) men walked like clumsy buffaloes, but that I had a graceful way of moving. I thanked her for her kind comments, wondering how the way I walked would influence the way I would speak Thai. How could there possibly be a connection? I was surprised, as time went by, to learn that in Thailand there was indeed a connection between the way one walked and the manner in which one talked. Everything in Thailand is about grace and charm. If you walk with grace, then you will probably speak with grace, and that's all that matters in the Land of Smiles. Some critics have been known to say that Thailand is mostly form and no substance, and I say to that, "So what? Would you rather live in Bangkok or Cleveland!" I think the answer is obvious.

There were two ways to get to my house. One route was to walk along Krung Kasem Road from the United Nations complex five minutes away, passing the flower market, the

Buddhist temple, and an abandoned palace with a graveyard of old school buses in its courtyard. Or you could take the Chao Phraya River Express that was a water taxi that plied the river from one end of Bangkok to the other. These water taxis were ancient, lurching, wooden craft that served as commuter transport for people living on tiny klongs, or canals, in Thon Buri that were fingers of the Chao Phraya River. A klong-dweller would travel first on a narrow long-tail boat and then transfer to the River Express and once again, probably have to take a bus or a tuk-tuk to wherever he was going. Since I worked in the United Nations building, my commute was a simple ten-minute walk; it could be a bit longer if I tarried in the market or went into the Buddhist temple to light a candle or sit for a minute and smell the incense and listen to the monks chanting.

My house was an interesting old pile of wood probably built at the beginning of the twentieth century in what I would call Javanese-New Orleans style. It was wrapped with a huge verandah, and the interior had fifteen-foot-high ceilings from which hung slow-moving fans that would stir the soupy humidity on sultry Bangkok afternoons. The front and back yards were shaded by old mango trees whose fruit would appear in March. My housekeeper would pick the almost-ripe mangoes from their branches before they fell or became prey to the ever-present crows, and put them in paper bags in the kitchen for a day or two until they were ripe. Then she would peel and slice them over sticky rice topped with coconut milk. This was the dessert of the hot dry season that lasted from March to May.

Bangkok had three seasons: the hot season was followed by the monsoon that lasted till the end of September. This was the time of year when the monks were supposed to stay in their monasteries and not walk about, trampling the newly planted paddi. Of course, times had changed and so had the land; most of what had been rice fields was now concrete. The cool season was my favorite and lasted from October till late February. Air-conditioners were turned off, and occasionally one might need a thin blanket at night. Suddenly, Bangkokians would appear on the street wearing sweaters, and the women would often have stylish little scarves wound around their necks; what constitutes cold for the Thais was a far cry from a New Yorker's definition of that condition.

In the middle of every rainy season, my yard would become flooded with ankle-deep tidal water coming in from the river. The first year this happened, I flew into a panic and was beside myself about having to wade out to the street every morning with my pants legs rolled up to the knee. The following year when the floods appeared again, I shrugged my shoulders, rolled up my trousers, and joined the other wet-footed pedestrians on the road in front of the Theves boat dock.

Learning and accepting were part of the Thai experience, just as was accepting the ever-present swarms of mosquitoes that appeared on my porch like clockwork every afternoon. My friend, Irma, who had been in Thailand for decades, told me to think of mosquito bites as kisses. I don't think I ever arrived at Irma's level of enlightenment in this regard, although well-oiled with Mekong whiskey, I might have thought of these attacks as love bites.

I found my house by chance and had to wait two years to move into it. It was inhabited by a foreign graduate student when I first visited the place. He said he had found it through the friend of a Thai friend and that he hated living there but stayed on because the rent was so cheap. No hot water, only one bathroom, water pressure so bad that it was almost impossible to take a shower. I took one look at the place and fell in love with it and knew I had to live there. I waited in a holding pattern, living in two other places until the scholar finished his dissertation and returned to Yale. I had no problem about the water pressure and the lack of hot water. Wrapped in a *pha kao ma*, my Thai sarong, I took a bath in the sunlight of the backyard every morning, dipping the cool water from a huge ceramic dragon jar with my beautiful silver bowl and splashing it over my head. I never tired of this refreshing ritual. I knew I could never be a Thai in this life, but bathing as they did was getting a bit closer to them.

I loved living in my house in Theves even though most of my friends likened it to a dilapidated, old Charles Addams mansion. I think I was one of the few *farang* who lived on the river. I knew of only one other European who had tried it, and his move had come to disaster. He lived in a small house on the edge of the water among working-class people who labored on the river or hawked food on the street. A non-Thai speaker, he was constantly robbed and was forced to move out to a more *farang*-friendly environment.

I think missionaries are probably the only people who can get away with going totally native, living among the masses in an alien culture. Other people, without a familiar mission, especially affluent UN employees as was the case with this young German, are suspected of some ulterior motive. To me, the fact that he was always being burgled did not so much indicate the inherent dishonesty of the Thais as much as it did his unfamiliarity with a Thai mindset that needed a reason to justify a stranger in their midst. *Why is he here with us? What does he want from us?* Unanswered, these questions lead to doubt and suspicion, which foment acts of rejection such as robbery or even worse.

Most of the expats lived in compounds or gated houses along Sukhumvit Road, near shopping centers and the international schools. I was single and had no such requirements. No kids to send to school and no need for frozen super market food when the bountiful local market, with its mouth-watering fresh produce, was just steps away from me. I had gone native, living among locals, but I lived in a secure compound guarded by police because my landlady's son was an army general.

I spent a lot of time just hanging out in my house, whose name was Baan Ban Tomsin. *Baan* in Thai is "house," and *Ban Tomsin* means "sleeping by the water." I liked it best when I was by myself. I would sit on my porch and absorb the sights and sounds of being on the river. Sometimes I would call the masseuse, an ancient, tiny, betel-chewing person from the dockside, to come to my house and give me a massage. She probably weighed eighty pounds, if that, but her hands were like steel. She carried a small tin can with her and would shoot a jet of betel spittle into it as she sat on the mat in my living room, kneading me with soothing but near-painful pressure from her thumbs. Sometimes when she left and I had paid her the twenty baht she demanded, I would see little drops of red, bloodlike betel juice on the polished teak floor.

The hum of river craft provided a pleasant, white-noise backdrop in the afternoon. In the evening when the buzz of market commerce had subsided, I heard the lonely voice of an old woman who had the tiniest of row boats, no bigger it seemed than a walnut shell. She cried out, "*Kam fak*—crossing to the other side," to advertise her water-taxi service to Thon Buri, a ten-minute paddle across the river. One night in the moonless, pitch dark, three of us managed to squeeze into her tiny craft for a trip to a house on stilts on the opposite side of the river where a Thai friend's foreign wife lived. She had lived so long in Thailand among the river people that she forgot how to speak English, and I was curious to meet somebody whom I might end up being like. I hoped I would.

Looking back, I see we were taking death into our hands traveling in this unlit, fly speck of a boat against the wake of huge teak rice barges and other speeding, motorized river traffic. The beautiful folly of youth never ceases to amaze me. Today, if you offered me all the tea in China I would not make such a trip again. It's like riding in helicopters. Today you wouldn't catch me in one of those machines for anything even though I logged hundreds of hours riding in choppers during the Vietnam War. I think there is a time to start doing things and a time to stop. You can just feel when that time has come, like when it is time to quit smoking or when you should stop getting drunk too often.

The spookiness of my place was particularly off-putting to Thais, who even before entering the door would look about and invariably say, "*Baan yai!*—Big house!" rolling their eyes with frowns on their foreheads. It was particularly difficult for me to retain housekeepers, who would take the job and then find some reason to quit. One lady, a particularly skilled housekeeper and gourmet cook, began to have seizures a few weeks after I engaged her.

I came home one afternoon and found her writhing on the kitchen floor, only the whites of her eyes showing. I was highly skeptical about her alleged malady, but I released her from our contract lest her "ailment" cost me a fortune. Later, I learned from her next employer that she thought the house was haunted and that I was a devil and that she had faked her illness as a way of getting away. It was all so Thai. Why not just tell me upfront that the house was too big or that the commute was too long and that it wasn't working out.

Confrontation and explanation are not part of the Thai mindset. During my time in Thailand, I saw many other cases when communication could have resolved issues, but other paths, even murderous ones, were taken instead. I consulted my Thai colleagues at the office, and they all said that no Thai wanted to work in a place that was lonely. In their highly collective society, lonely is a really frightening concept to people who have no appreciation for solitude or being on one's own.

I finally found a woman who did not seem bothered by living in a Charles Addams house. She arrived one day on the recommendation of another servant who heard I was looking for help. She was not alone. Chained to her suitcase was a large black dog with the name of Meck, which means "cloud" in Thai. I realized after a few weeks that Orn was illiterate. I would jot down items we needed for the kitchen and give her the shopping list to take to the market. She always returned with a variety of purchases that was at odds with what I thought I had asked for. When I said, "But where's the bread?" she would say, "They're out of it," or "It was too expensive and I decided not to buy it this time." The clincher came when I saw her looking at my list, holding it upside down. It didn't really matter to me whether she could read or not. She was a good person and seemed devoted to me, and I liked Meck, who lived quietly in the servants' quarters.

Although I made no effort to improve the condition of the house—truth be told, it was beyond repair—I did improve the garden with numerous plantings, including a beautiful flower-bearing tulip tree. My landlady, who lived opposite me, often saw me toiling in the garden and suggested I get a gardener. She said that a white gentleman had no business mucking about in the dirt. "What would the neighbors say?" she asked me. She intimated, being a titled lady, that she only wanted to rent to quality folks and that did not include people who, God forbid, mucked around in a garden!

I agreed heartily with her, laughing to myself about who *she* really was. My secretary, a member of the Thai aristocracy, told me that my landlady and her sister had come to Thailand from China as a teenaged prostitutes in the twenties. Because of her great beauty, her luminous complexion, and her facility for entertainment—she was reputed for her skill at playing the lute while cracking melon seeds with her teeth and passing the seeds mouth-to-mouth to her client—she rose rapidly in Thai society and had married a nobleman who was the king's paramour. She was later in the Bangkok tabloids in the thirties for being involved in a "crime de passion" when she murdered her lover in a jealous quarrel.

So I heeded the advice of my landlady-cum-murderous-prostitute with the perfect ivory skin and hired a gardener who was a relative of one of her staff. I never liked the man from the beginning, but I tolerated him because Orn seemed happy to have another person living in the vast, empty servants' quarters, and it was always good to have an extra pair of hands around the house, especially during flood season.

What put me off was that this gardener did not really act like a Thai but more like an American redneck from Alabama, a loud-mouthed swaggerer who had none of the natural grace and class that almost all Thais possess. As far as I knew, he was honest and hardworking, but I just didn't like him. His noisiness got to me.

One evening when I was reading on the verandah, I was disturbed by what sounded like drunken hoots coming from the servants' quarters. I decided to find out what all the uproar was about and tiptoed outside and down the front steps to where they lived. I stood for a few minutes eavesdropping on their conversation—actually more a monologue from the gardener—and realized that even though they were speaking an upcountry dialect of Thai, they were making fun of me. I heard the gardener mimic my voice when I called Orn in the morning to bring me a cup of tea or a coffee. What really hurt me was her laughing at his impersonation.

I realized that she may have been a captive audience and that they were simple people who needed their jobs, but my pride and arrogance got the best of me and I fired them. I fired the gardener outright, saying that I didn't need him anymore. With Orn, I took her aside in the living room and told her that I felt I had been insulted by somebody I liked and I could not live with that situation. She cried and said she understood, and then she packed her bags and left the next morning, with Meck trailing behind. I watched as they walked down the lane by the Buddhist temple, her back bent over with the weight of her cheap cardboard luggage and Meck, frightened by the traffic, tugging at his chain.

I almost called out to tell her to come back, but I didn't. I often wonder what happened to them and find myself regretting my impulsive, egotistical act. I realized that I was turning into a haughty, over-sensitive neo-colonialist; such was the way of the white man in the Asian tropics. It seemed to happen to all of us in one way or another. I hoped I could become a good Buddhist and a better person and not let my ego spoil things for myself and those with whom I associated.

Not far from my house, a few steps down Krung Kasem Road was a residential compound owned by an upper-class Thai family. I had become friendly with the inhabitants who included Khunying Saisuri and her husband, Khun Kamling. Lady Saisuri was one of the most delightful, unaffected people I had ever met and her husband was a statuesque, handsome gentleman, a Thai version of Errol Flynn. It was therefore with great surprise that I viewed a photo thirty years later of two very obese people, one wheelchair-bound, both dressed in mournful black garments. The person who showed me the picture asked if I knew who this couple was, and after staring at the photo for a couple of minutes, I said I had no idea. It was Lady Saisuri and her husband, Khun Kamling, he said! I was shocked and saddened that they had become so deformed and unrecognizable. With every possible privilege and resource at their disposal, why had this happened to them? They could have had an army of personal trainers; they could have jogged or walked at their leisure at the Royal Bangkok Sports Club or other watering holes for the privileged. It seemed every day I was struck by examples of the truth that Buddhism expounded, and in this case, looking at that photo, I saw how transitory our human lives are and how nothing ever remains the same.

Although I came to love the total package that was Thai culture, I found certain elements of Thai society repugnant and objectionable. To me the most attractive aspects of Thai life were represented by the "common" people; the simplest, poorest farmers and workers possessed a grace and natural dignity that I seldom saw in people outside of Southeast Asia until I went to Mexico years later. In contrast, I often found the Thai upper-class spoiled and arrogantly invested with self-entitlement, not worthy of the noble titles attached to their ornate, long names. Nothing turned me off as much as hearing a "khunying" (titled lady) hiss an order to her servant in acid tones covered with a patina of phony velvet. And I could never reconcile myself to that Thai custom of groveling whereby persons of "lower station" would cringe in the presence of their "superiors" by lowering themselves physically to a level below the head and shoulders of the "revered" one. Try as I would to accept these practices, the best I could do was to shrug to myself and say, "Different strokes for different folks."

Farther down the road was my office, the United Nations, located in an impressive high-rise building surrounded by flame trees that bloomed spectacularly during the hot season. The chief of mission, my boss, was a pretentious, bossy ogre of a man from Boston, and I got off on the wrong foot with him from day one. I had arrived from New York to take up my job, and as my first duty the second day of work, I was told to join him for a meeting. We got in his chauffeur-driven car, which had been air-conditioned to the point of bone-chilling coldness. After a minute or two, I began shaking uncontrollably while he looked at me as though I were going mad. I realized, being obese, that he had a layer of insulation I did not possess and therefore could tolerate the cold, but this was more than I could bear. He then thrust a fat file at me and said, "Read this!"

I have always avoided reading while riding in a moving vehicle because I become violently nauseous if I put my eyes on a written page while in motion. So there I was, freezing to death with my teeth clacking, trying not to vomit and, at the same time, absorb the meaning of an arcane budget about government counterpart contributions to the project we were about to meet on and discuss. Luckily this miscreant, who was disliked intensely by his Thai counterparts, left Bangkok in a few months and was replaced by a fun-loving, laid-back Filipino who adored me.

In fact, he liked me so much that I sensed other staff members had become jealous. We used to travel all around the country together on project visits, and his favorite junkets were trips to the beautiful northern city of Chiang Mai. I knew when he wanted to make a trip to Chiang Mai. He would ring me on the phone and simply say, "Sam, Number 34!" cackle loudly and hang up. Number 34 referred to the number of the masseuse in his favorite massage parlor, and I was always detailed to set up their appointments. I was not thrilled in my role as procurer, but at least it beat freezing to death and being nauseated.

I realize now, years later, how honest and naïve I was back then. As international civil servants, we UN employees had very attractive benefits that allowed us generous duty-free importation of luxury goods. The most attractive perk was the right to import any type of foreign automobile into Thailand, a very protected market where locals were compelled to pay crushing import taxes for Mercedes-Benzes and other up-market motor car models. At that time, a Benz might have cost $25,000 for us to import duty-free. On the Thai open market, they retailed for over $100,000.

Every year, most of my colleagues were importing expensive cars and selling them to rich Chinese merchants for $80,000, thereby realizing an extra $55,000 per year, almost the equivalent of a mid-level officer's salary at that time. Had I been wiser, I could, with perfect legality, have imported five cars during my tour of duty in Thailand and salted away nearly $300,000, a considerable amount of money back in the seventies. But I had no interest in either owning a car myself or doing what I considered such dirty business. Sadder but wiser is what we become. If I had the choice today, I would not have hesitated one second.

I often thought about our efforts and their effect on developing countries when I worked with the United Nations Development Program in Thailand and in other places where I was assigned. In Thailand, I was convinced we were doing good work that directly benefitted the population. We were engaged in supporting bread-and-butter development projects that involved agricultural productivity, primary health care, educational innovation, family planning, and urban sanitation. Those were the kinds of undertakings that could be measured for success and monitored meaningfully for improvement.

Today, development programs are much more "upstream" and deal with broad issues, such as good governance, the elimination of corruption, and the promotion of women's rights. While such causes may be admirable, I feel it is inadvisable for an external aid agency to impose its will on a host country in these areas of national life. Not only is it difficult to realize specific success in such undertakings, it places the donor agency in a neo-colonial role where outside perspectives are imposed on indigenous cultures. I realize that these statements may be shocking and unacceptable to well-meaning, politically correct people, but I think my experience has shown my opinions to be correct.

Thankfully, I am now retired from the UN and do not have to deal with these upstream pipe dreams. In recent years, I was called back to my old office to carry out several consultancies that involved analyzing the success of recent projects and programs, and based on that experience and the anecdotal evidence of others, I feel convinced that development agencies should turn back the clock and revert to old-fashioned development concepts: fertilizer, inoculations, teacher training.

The United Nations Regional Commission for Asia and the Pacific (ESCAP) occupied most of the glistening high-rise building near my home in Theves. Thousands of staff were employed there, and I never managed to get a handle on what they were doing that was specifically, measurably useful for the developing world. I realized that diplomatic necessity required a forum for the interchange of ideas and problems among nations, but the plethora of meetings, conferences, workshops, study tours, and, most of all, mountains of reports convinced me, in all seriousness, that it would be preferable to close down 90 percent of the Regional Commission's activities. The money that would be saved by such a drastic and obviously impossible action could be simply air-dropped throughout Thailand and the neighboring countries from helicopters and would result in more good done than the snoring in five languages that was the modus operandi for ESCAP and its Mercedes-trafficking staff members.

With a mixture of regret and excitement, I left Thailand after five years for a new assignment in neighboring Burma. I was eager to see what lay across the border in a country that had been shut off from the world for a generation and where time had virtually stopped. I would not be disappointed.

CHAPTER NINE

BENTOTA DREAMING
When Sri Lanka Was a Magical Place

Several months ago, a small package wrapped in plain brown paper was delivered to my house. I scarcely noticed it when I got home, sitting inconspicuously among the other accumulated detritus on my kitchen table. But I did detect a tangy perfume wafting about the room and eventually traced the odor to this modest object. My name and address were scribbled on the front of the package, and it was stamped with postage from Sri Lanka. Also stamped on the front of the box was the notation: "Insufficient Postage— Return to Sender." A piece of white paper with a note was wedged under the string wrapped around the parcel. It was from my friend, Tony, who lived in Toronto, and said, "Here is some tea from Trevor. He thinks of you and the wonderful times you spent together in Ceylon and wishes you could come back again someday for a visit."

It had been twenty-five years or more since I had been to Sri Lanka and a good ten years since Trevor and I had been in contact. Trevor was Trevor Roose Male-Cocq, a Sri Lankan Burgher of European extraction, who worked for George Stewart Company. I was touched that an old friend would have remembered me and gone to the trouble of sending what turned out to be a packet of my favorite Ceylon breakfast tea. Trevor's mother had always served it to us in the afternoon when I visited their place in Colombo. Seeing the little box and smelling its contents brought back memories of civilized conversation and warm companionship.

I thought fondly of my salad days and the visits I had made to Ceylon. That was the nostalgic name for the teardrop-shaped country now known as Sri Lanka. I called my friend in Toronto to thank him for delivering the tea. He said he had passed through New York, returning from a trip to Asia, and while there he had had the opportunity to visit Sri Lanka and look up Trevor. I had introduced them some years ago, and they had developed a friendship. It was part of that network of relationships that traveling Asia hands tend to develop, sharing names of people, likeminded souls, who later become good friends.

Tony told me that Trevor, who was only in his late fifties, had developed an early case of Alzheimer's disease. He had his good moments interspersed with long lapses into vagueness. Tony said that when he visited, Trevor had been his old self and had talked animatedly about the good old days. Of course, my name came up during the conversation about the goings-on of our gang of friends back in the seventies, and before Tony departed, Trevor asked him to deliver the box of tea to me. He told Tony that it had been returned to him and he didn't know how he could get it to me.

I was deeply touched and saddened by what had happened to Trevor. The last time I had seen him, we had gone to the beach in Bentota on the south coast down from Colombo. His cricket equipment was in the trunk of the car, and once we got down to the water's edge, he began bowling cricket pitches to a friend whom he had run into on the beach by chance and hadn't seen since school days. The joyous reunion of these two men, suddenly becoming boys again, was a lovely sight, and I filed that image in my memory bank as the way I wanted to remember Trevor: running like a zephyr, shouting, smiling, sweating, and hugging his friend with loving gusto at the end of their impromptu, salty cricket match; now he sat in an easy chair in his mum's living room, staring vacantly out the window all day. *Sic Transit Gloria.*

Try as I will, I cannot remember exactly how I came to know Sri Lanka. It was in the mid-seventies that I started going there, and I must have had an introduction to Trevor from somebody in the Asia hands network. In any case, I recall being told that Sri Lanka was a good place to go for a holiday and being posted in not-so-far-away Thailand, I went for my Christmas holiday one year. I checked into the fabled Galle Face Hotel, a colonial pile of ruined splendor perched on the edge of the crashing waves of the Indian Ocean.

Barefooted attendants padded silently along polished hallways, bearing silver trays loaded with high tea, and cawing black crows snitched anything left on my table on the hotel room balcony. Later, when I got to know the family, Trevor's mother told me how to get rid of those pesky birds. Just shine a mirror at them when they landed and they would flee as quickly as a vampire seeing a crucifix, she said. She led me to the garden to demonstrate, taking her makeup compact from her pocket, opening it, and flashing the mirror at the first blackbird that landed. Away he went as soon as the mirror caught the light and refracted back into his beady little eyes. I got a little mirror and tried it and it worked like a charm. And it was fun, too, to chase away those ugly, Hitchcockian, feathered things.

My first encounter with Trevor took place when I called on him in his office at George Stewart Company located in the historic Fort neighborhood of Colombo. George Stewart was an ancient trading company founded in the seventeenth century by Burghers, the European settler-traders who preceded the British who later made Ceylon a colony. The building and its interior had a museumlike quality, as did the Fort, the oldest section of Colombo, where Dutch traders first established their factories and businesses.

We chatted and agreed to meet that evening at my hotel. Over dinner, I impressed Trevor with my ability to eat string hoppers that were laced with a fiery gravy that made Ceylonese food the spiciest in the world. I told him I got my training in my birthplace, New Orleans, when my mother would add a drop of Tabasco chili-sauce to my glasses of milk when I was a child. In a display of hospitality that I would later find to be almost universal in Sri Lankan society, Trevor invited me to move out of the hotel and come stay with him and his family in their home.

I could relate easily to this spontaneous display of hospitality to a near-stranger because I came from New Orleans, where inviting people home for dinner whom you had just met on the street was par for the course. He said there was plenty of room and explained that his parents would love the company. His father had retired some years before as head of the Sri Lankan policy force and was an amiable gentleman who liked to talk about his time as the country's chief law-enforcer.

Trevor added that with visitors coming and going all day long, I would have the chance to meet an interesting cross-section of Ceylonese society and get to know the country. Without thinking twice, I accepted his kind offer. Thus began my happy connection with Trevor and his parents, whom I came to regard as my own family.

On Friday when Trevor got back home from the office, he suggested we make a weekend trip to Bentota to visit his friend, Bevis Bawa, who had a farm named Brief. Trevor said Bevis was fond of alliteration and reveled in the words on his calling card that read: "Bevis Bawa, Brief, Bentota." The next morning we drove south towards Galle down the palm-lined, two-lane coastal road with the ocean to our right and the smell of salt water in the air. At one point, we stopped for a break and a leg-stretch to imbibe in the sweet water from fresh, young coconuts and to watch the fishermen, perched on poles way out at sea. When we arrived at Brief and entered its gate, climbing up the long driveway, we saw an immensely tall figure standing on the front steps of the columned porch, waving towards us.

It was Bevis. Bevis stood six foot four and must have weighed no more than 160 pounds. Dressed in Singhalese traditional attire—a loose, light cotton shirt, silk sarong, his head capped with what looked like a cross between a kepi and a turban—Bevis greeted us warmly and in impeccable British English, decorated with ever-so-upper-class round tones, asked us how our trip had been. Over an endless lunch, well-watered with arak, the fiery Sri Lankan coconut liquor, we feasted on a cloyless array of native dishes, the contents of which came from Bevis's farm.

Bevis was a gentleman farmer in the old style, but he was also a serious agriculturalist who was experimenting with different varieties of plantation crops and helping local farmers propagate these new varieties to improve their livelihoods. Bevis was also a bit of an eccentric. His bathroom was located to the side of his bedroom, and the commode was built in such a way that he could sit on it and, concealed waist-down by a Dutch half-door, look out onto the courtyard where his staff had assembled to receive their work orders for the day.

This was his daily routine, sitting on the john at seven in the morning with a cup of his home-grown coffee in hand, giving out marching orders for the day's tasks. His farm, spread out in hacienda fashion, had groves of coffee, cocoa, cloves, pepper, and other tropical crops, and his vast courtyard became a veritable art gallery when yards of colorful harvest were spread out to dry in the sun on finely-woven reed mats.

There were brown coffee beans, red and green chilies, maroon cloves, rust-colored sticks of cinnamon, and pearly sheaves of freshly harvested rice fanned out like strokes on an artist's palette, all of which had inspired a famous Australian painter to cover the walls of Bevis's home with colorful murals and frescoes depicting life as it was lived at Brief. I spent many weekends at Brief becoming a regular guest and one of Bevis's inner circle. I also got to know his equally tall brother, Geoffrey, a brilliant architect who had designed the breathtakingly beautiful new Sri Lankan parliament building.

The son of a fabulously wealthy Arab merchant who had married a French countess and settled in Ceylon, Bevis was raised in an atmosphere of privilege. But like a true aristocrat, he was simple and unpretentious and had that extraordinary ability, common only to greatly gifted politicians and princes born to the manor, of seeming interested in you and you alone when you were in his presence.

In Bevis's case, it was genuine. He had spent his youth as an entitled young rake, riding about Colombo in his chauffeur-driven Rolls Royce and, having duly sown his oats, had now become a serious farmer. He had everything money could buy except one thing: Vivien Leigh. Bevis was greatly enamored of this glamorous creature ever since she had starred in *Gone with the Wind*. He was therefore beside himself when he learned, sometime in the early fifties, that Miss Leigh was in town, having come to Colombo to star in *Elephant Walk*, a steamy tropical adventure film featuring a swash-buckling plantation owner, his gorgeous wife, and herds of snorting, stamped-ing elephants.

Biding his time, Bevis racked his brain about the best way of meeting Miss Leigh. As a leading member of Colombo society, he would have had no problem getting a proper introduction to the actress, but this was not Bevis's style. He had plotted something better, something more stylish, more Bevis. Since he knew the Ceylonese crew working on the film, which was to be shot on location near Brief, Bevis was informed of Vivien's daily schedule and had memorized her comings and goings, plotted down to her every movement.

She was staying at the Galle Face Hotel and, it ap-peared, had tea every afternoon at four o'clock in the lobby; for Vivien, "tea" was her habitual pink gin of which she was becoming overly fond. Bevis managed to be in the lobby every afternoon at four, sometimes dressed in a white linen suit topped with a Borsalino, other times costumed in rav-ishing Singhalese silks of heavenly hues. The cat and mouse game had begun.

Impossible to ignore, Bevis would avoid her gaze, pre-tending she was not there while others in the lobby were swarming to say hello and beg for an autograph. This tan-talizing dance went on for a week or more. Then one day Vivien got up from her rattan lounge chair, and with pink gin in hand, walked over to Bevis, who was gazing out at the Indian Ocean pretending to be deep in thought. She confronted him in her best Scarlett O'Hara style: "Sir, you are the most terrible person. For days I have been dying to speak with you, but you ignore me like I am the plague! Am I that horrible?"

It didn't take long for the pair to become the fastest of friends. They could be seen every afternoon riding through Colombo's stylish neighborhoods in his Rolls Royce, their faces bending close to each other in the deepest of conversations. Filming of *Elephant Walk* churned on, and Vivien, bored with the routine of shooting and early morning wake-up calls, took increasingly to her pink gins.

Tongues were also beginning to wag about Colombo's most eligible bachelor and England's most famous film star. The tongues had wagged so loudly that word about their gallivanting about town reached London and Vivien's husband, Laurence Olivier. Insanely jealous, Olivier descended on Colombo and snatched Vivien from the film set and from what he thought were the amorous arms of Bevis.

More than halfway completed, production of the film was thrown into chaos without its star. Eventually, Elizabeth Taylor was called in to replace Vivien, and the picture was finally completed. Apparently, Larry Olivier was never told that Bevis was as gay as a box of birds. It later turned out that Olivier was of that persuasion, too. His flaming affair with Danny Kaye was recently recounted in a best-seller that described Vivien often answering the phone, frown on her face, and then passing the receiver to Olivier and saying, "It's him again!" Strange are the ways of the glamorous and famous.

Trevor's friends were not all glamorous Rolls Royce own-
ers. He had befriended a hippy Dutchman who was a poet
and a painter but looked more like a bookkeeper. He lived
in a tiny room in the working-class section of Colombo and
invited us to tea one day. The tea was elaborately prepared
over a campfire single-burner gas stove, and Hans' "teacups"
were old baked bean tins he had salvaged from the garbage
and washed off. The tin's lids were still attached to the tops
and hung over like tongues and were used as handles.

He gave us tiny sections of toilet paper to insulate our
fingers from the scalding metal and served us some tired little
biscuits on sections of cardboard. I found this rustic hospitality

to be charming and genuine. Hans told us that he was only living in Colombo in this primitive state until he could build his dream house under a coconut tree in a village near the beach. He said he had already chosen the spot. He promised to invite us when his dream manse had been completed.

A year or so later, when I inquired about Hans, Trevor told me that the Dutchman's plan had turned into a disaster. After moving to the village and building his dream house, tensions with the villagers began to arise. It seemed the Dutchman could not accustom himself to rural Sri Lankan life. The culture of collective living was alien to him. When neighbors borrowed his tools and ate the fruit from the trees in his garden, he threatened them.

With the constant drumbeat of village festivals that lasted for days on end, Hans would cover his ears and scream at the "savages." Trevor visited Hans once and cautioned him that *he* was the guest and had to learn to adapt to the culture of the village and not vice-versa. Hans had told us that he hated the Western colonial mentality, but when Trevor pointed out to him that he himself was acting out what he had condemned, Hans told Trevor that he was racist.

Several weeks afterward, Trevor's father heard from his police sources that the remains of a European's body had been found hacked to death on the beach near Galle. We later learned that it was Hans. The clash between modern lifestyle and traditional culture plays itself out in many ways and in various locations with a multitude of different actors. Usually because of their wealth and power, Westerners prevail, but not always.

The massive movement of people across frontiers and cultures has become a leading theme in twenty-first-century life. How it will play itself out is anyone's guess. A melting pot can become a murderous cauldron if social engineering and mass emotion take the wrong direction. Sri Lanka itself is just now emerging from more than three decades of communal strife with great loss of life. It is not an exaggeration to say that the country had come close to self-destruction. It is anybody's guess whether one of the most beautiful, blessed places in the world will rise from the ashes or sink again into strife. RIP, Hans.

Over a period of more than ten years, I visited Sri Lanka many times, often traveling with Trevor and other friends or sometimes making trips on my own. Sri Lanka retained many features of its colonial heritage. Among them was the network of circuit houses established during the time of the Raj to accommodate visiting district officers on inspection tours of the countryside. These cozy, rather basic accommodations could be found almost everywhere and provided welcoming stopover points for travelers willing to pay the equivalent of a few dollars per night.

For the price, guests would be given a spotless room, wide beds always furnished with a "Dutch Wife"—a three-foot-long tubular pillow—an ear-splitting bang on the door at 5:30 a.m. with the arrival of a white-suited attendant bearing a cup of "bed tea" so deadly strong that a teaspoon would stand upright in the cup and a plate of cold, rock-hard toast served *a l'anglais* filed in a silver-plated toast carrier. I have many fond memories of these picturesque little circuit houses so redolent of times gone by.

There were memorable excursions to Kandy, one of the truly exquisite places on earth and a trip to Trincomalee, a beautiful port town on the northeast coast, later to be destroyed in the battles between Tamils and Singhalese. Trevor's family had a beach house on the outskirts of Trinco. One night when we were staying there, we walked on the beach at sunset watching the fishing boats come in from the sea. As the sun sank behind the horizon, small fires were lit all along the shoreline, casting long shadows as the men toiled with their nets, and the freshest of little fish, just caught, were grilled on tiny charcoal braziers by the fishermen's wives and daughters. Squatting on the sand, native-style and barefooted, we ate the exquisite catch, and I came as close as I ever would to becoming a Sri Lankan.

Of all the Asian lands I have known and visited, Sri Lanka more than any other country—even more than India or the Philippines—seems to have an affinity for Westerners. I found myself feeling truly at home in Sri Lanka. Perhaps its gentle Buddhism was the answer. If so, how could a country become convulsed in violence and conflict as it had for so many decades? Outside interference from the Tamils of South India is often blamed for the murderous war. Who can say for sure?

Although I sometimes passed the UN office on my walkabouts around Colombo, I never actually went in to pay a visit. I knew from my work in other duty stations that the last thing a busy field office needed was a visiting "fireman" from another UN office coming to mooch a cup of coffee and ask where the best restaurants were and whether the water was safe to drink.

My disinclination to look in on the Colombo office was greatly increased when I heard that the chief of mission, a nutty Dutchman, had decided in a back-to-the-soil, cultural revolutionary stroke of genius to dig up the office's beautiful garden and replace the bowers of orchids and stands of sweet jasmine with irrigated trenches that grew corn and barley, crops that Sri Lankans did not eat in any case. The UN was full of incompetent know-it-alls who couldn't succeed in their own countries but had managed somehow to foist themselves on countries who needed them even less.

If Bevis were alive today, he would be nearly one hundred years old. We stayed in touch into the eighties, and once I mailed him a beautiful magenta-colored Thai silk dressing gown from Bangkok. He sent me a gracious thank you note scrawled in almost illegible handwriting saying that because he was almost blind, he couldn't see what I had sent him very well, but the feel of the material was "smashing" and the rustle of the silk rather "naughty." I hate to think what might have happened to Brief after Bevis's death. He had no heirs other than his servants. I hope the land and the house were divided amongst them and that they are still living happily at Brief, farming the way Bevis would have wanted.

My supply of Ceylon tea is growing short, and I have decided to stretch out what is left, that I may have one cup of tea per month. I will sit in my kitchen drinking the tea, look out the window at my garden, and try to imagine that Trevor and I are in his parents' house and that his mum is serving us tea. Who knows? When I have finished my supply of Ceylon Breakfast, maybe another fragrant little box will arrive.

❧【CHAPTER TEN】❧

PAY BYOKE!
Burmese Mornings

For most of the year, mornings were my favorite time in Burma. Especially during the hot, dry season that lasted from February to mid-May, when the sky opened and monsoon rains began their deluge, the early daylight hours were the most pleasant. The air was fresh and not yet oven-hot. One could walk down the middle of the roads and lanes of Rangoon, encountering hardly a soul—only single files of barefooted, red-robed Buddhist monks on their rounds for morning alms and food, their black lacquer begging bowls held in both hands as they stopped to receive food and donations from housewives standing on the road, ladling out pungent curry and rice from large pots.

And there was always the pay byoke lady. Pay byoke was a morning food consisting of steamed peas that was sold by women who plied the lanes of residential neighborhoods from the crack of dawn. To keep warm, the peas were wrapped in a towel and were further insulated inside a square reed basket that was balanced on the head of the pay byoke lady as she moved from house to house, crying out her sing-song call, "Pay byoke!" I loved seeing her come down my road, smoking a pungent cheroot and adjusting the load on her head.

Burmese carried many things on their heads that we would normally hold in our hands. During the rainy season, when the downpours stopped, Burmese would roll up their umbrellas and balance them on their heads. I always had a déjà vu moment when I heard the pay byoke lady's melodious voice cut the air, and it was only after a few months that I realized the sound was almost identical to the call of the chimney sweep in the New Orleans of my childhood. "Ramoner, ramoner! Do you have any chimneys to sweep today?" Vendors' cries had disappeared from the life of American cities. It was somehow comforting to find survivors in far away Burma.

There was much from the past that had survived in Burma. I lived in Rangoon in the late seventies and early eighties, and I could say that time there had stopped; the clock simply seemed to have ceased ticking in Burma. A military dictatorship had seized power from a chaotic but democratic government in 1960, and a strange political arrangement called Burmese Socialism had taken over.

Capitalism withered, and economic growth stagnated. Ancient motor cars and buses plied the potholed avenues, and mashed grains of rice were used to glue postage stamps onto letters. At night, there was virtually no illumination in the city, and old automobiles staggered down the road with no headlights. Reading George Orwell's *Burmese Days* was like perusing the morning paper. Physically and mentally, Burma remained the sleepy, provincial, colonial land it had been in the thirties. The English were gone, but a new form of colonial exploitation by the Burmese military had taken their place.

I was a great fan of pay byoke and would have it most mornings with smokey Shan tea or sometimes a cup of strong Burmese coffee. Pay byoke could be eaten any way but was tastiest with warm naan bread or rice. Most foreigners had not heard of pay byoke, and I was proud that I had discovered this delicious secret.

The other culinary treasure I discovered was mohingga, another morning dish roughly equivalent to bouillabaisse, but with tropical modifications including hearts of young banana tree trunks chopped up in the soup. There was an infinite variety of mohingga to be found in Rangoon, and I became an expert in all of the best places. I would squat-sit on a tiny stool a foot off the sidewalk and indulge in this matinal gourmet delight.

My home in Rangoon was an apartment in a rather functional, drab-looking building that contained four units and sat behind a wall on a quiet lane called Budd Road. Budd must have been some minor British colonial hero or middling English functionary, and the Burmese had simply forgotten to change the street's name to something local, probably because of its insignificance.

I had decided to take this accommodation, which was the very opposite of what I had lived in when I worked in Bangkok before coming to Rangoon on assignment.

In Bangkok, I had lived in a sprawling, old wooden house on the river that was totally open and could not have been secured against burglars. I had heard that because of the high level of poverty in Burma, and also because I was single and would be living alone, an apartment would be more appropriate for me.

The Burmese were not inherently dishonest people. They were just desperately poor, and robbing a bit from a rich foreigner was not considered sinful—rather, it was Robin Hood-esque and to be expected. The only problem was, Burma did not have any flats except for a few embassy residences for singles, and I could not qualify for such quarters since I was not a diplomat belonging to a particular country. It turned out there was one place, the Budd Road flat, but I would have to wait some time before I could get it.

I cooled my heels for three months in the Inya Lake Hotel, a huge, gloomy accommodation that had been built in the fifties as one of the showcase Soviet aid projects in Burma. Pure Stalin was the style, and the food was just as grim. After weeks of eating mostly cabbage and potatoes, I began to assume a pasty-faced look. That started my exploration for other eating options, and I discovered the panoply of foods that could be found in the city: Chinese, Indian, Shan and old-style British colonial. The Inya Lake Hotel was an interesting place where all manner of people collided. Burma's declared policy of neutrality had attracted representation from almost all countries, including North Korea and East Germany, both of which had huge embassies in Rangoon.

There were always large delegations from the DPKR, Democratic Peoples' Republic of Korea, and I would watch them with fascination as they marched in tight formation, two by two, into the hotel dining room, their faces frozen and eyes pointed ahead of them in a tunnel vision, Manchurian candidate focus. They didn't eat from the normal hotel menu and had special dishes that looked like Chinese food prepared for them.

Once when I was waiting at the entrance to the dining room, I caught one of the Korean's attention and made eye contact. I smiled and blurted out the only Korean words I knew: "An yang!" or hello! In return I got the most withering glance I had ever seen. I now know what pure, unadulterated hate looks like. To paraphrase a song, "If looks could kill, I'd be dead on arrival." This fleeting moment of non-rapport made an assignment I was given some weeks later a particularly challenging task.

My boss ordered me to make an appointment with the North Korean Embassy to discuss their aid program to Burma. The United Nations served as umbrella coordinating agency for the donor community and was charged with producing an annual compendium of contributions. My job: collect the data. The appointment with an embassy first secretary seemed to proceed normally enough. Then came the moment for refreshments. As a glass of orange soda was proffered me, I thought to myself, *To drink or not to drink? This may be the most important decision of my life.* I threw caution to the winds and quaffed the liquid and was none the worse for it. Thus began my warm relationship with the DPKR!

I settled into my flat and was lucky to find a house-keeper who was both honest and pleasant, if a bit limited in his culinary abilities. Sein was an older man from the Karen tribe. This ethnic group, almost all of them Christian, had been in open rebellion against the Burmese for more than a generation, as had other tribes, notably the Shan, who shared a culture and a language close to the Thais.

Sein was a wizard at making Western breakfasts and cooked one dish that I had never seen before. It involved an egg and a piece of bread. The bread was fried in a pan as one would do as if making French toast, but in this case a square of the bread was removed from the middle and an egg was cracked into it. The result was a delicious fusion of French toast and fried egg. For other meals, Sein had a repertoire of about half a dozen dishes that he would serve again and again. I got bored with tuna casserole, baked beans, and his one version of Indian curry and began picking at my dinner. The result was my losing weight to the point of becoming truly skinny. I was nearly six feet tall and weighed less than 150 pounds.

Although I never had any major problems with break-ing and entering as did other expats in Rangoon who lived in large, open houses, I did have one interesting experience with a diamond stick (*sein taju*) burglar. The diamond stick technique involved a long, light-weight pole, not unlike an elongated fishing rod, with a hook affixed to the end. This protuberance could reach through a small space in a win-dow and scoop up valuable baubles lying a few feet away on a table or bureau. Hence the name diamond stick. In my case, it was a Rolex watch that got nabbed when the dia-mond stick went fishing. Undeterred by the window's metal security bars, a neat little Caesarian section slit was made in my bedroom window's screen, and the wrist watch was surgically removed from my bedside night stand while I was enjoying an afternoon siesta!

I decided to go native, sartorially speaking, and began to wear the Burmese sarong or longyi. Alone in Southeast Asia, Burmese, male and female, eschew Western dress, preferring their handsome and practical local clothing. For men, once you get the knack of tying it securely and attractively, making a nice knot with a tongue of cloth protruding as kind of a fashion statement, the longyi is easy, comfortable, and nice-looking to wear. It is worn with a cotton shirt, and depending on the formality of the occasion, jackets are included. Typically men did not wear anything under the longyi, so maximum ventilation was achieved, as was the ability to engage in and retreat from a quick tryst.

Wearing a sarong also required wearing the native footwear, sandals, which took a bit of breaking in and a number of blisters between big and second toe before I was comfortable abandoning my shoes. I was surprised how versatile I became with the sandals, and after a couple of years I was able to go on mountain hikes wearing them. The only problem with most Western men and sandals is aesthetic. Caucasian feet tend to be long, bony, and ugly, and the sandal exposes this podiatric defect in "round-eyes." Nonetheless, I wore native garb for nearly five years, and when it came time for me to move to my next assignment, Indonesia, I found I no longer had a proper Western wardrobe. That was not to be a problem in Jakarta, where batik shirts were de rigueur.

Although I studied the Burmese language assiduously and learned to read, write, and speak it to a fairly good level of fluency, I never took to it as I did to Thai, a reputedly more difficult language due to its five tones. Spoken Burmese, to me, was not a beautiful language to listen to and sounded very slurred to my ear. It was also spoken very rapidly. I only recall a few Burmese people I knew who spoke it in what I considered a pleasing manner.

Burmese, men in particular, tended to shout when they spoke, and their conversation was accompanied by rather violent body language and gestures very much akin to Indians. Burmese food was also a sister of Indian cuisine and was characterized by being extremely oily, although many dishes, such as mohingga, were delicious as well as healthy. Carrying the linguistic-culinary parallel to the people, I found Burmese more like Indians than Southeast Asians.

They are extremely hierarchically oriented and tend to assume groveling, obsequious attitudes when in the company of people they fancy to be their superiors. It was funny with the language; I seem to have forgotten most of the Burmese I learned, whereas with Thai, I still speak it without any problem.

Left on their own and operating in environments where they were at their ease, Burmese were charming and naturally friendly. Probably one of the most handsome races in Southeast Asia, Burmese women were statuesque, and the average girl with a basket on her head hawking in the market could compete with any runway model; Burmese men were usually handsome and manlier than their Thai or Vietnamese counterparts.

By now I had worked in a number of UN field offices and was used to the cast of characters, international and local, that one found in our operations. Expats came and went, and the locals were aware of the ephemeral nature of the international presence. As with any group of people, there were the capable ones and the less capable ones among the foreign staff. Expatriates were usually posted to Burma for two to four years maximum. How much impact one chief of mission could have during his or her limited tenure was questionable, especially when the necessity of adhering to the inclination of the host government put a serious damper on any radical policy departure that would have been contemplated. Still, taking certain useful initiatives was within the power of the UN resident representative.

At the beginning of the eighties, the advent of widespread computer use in offices was occurring. Our office in Rangoon had not yet become computerized, so it was with a good deal of positive anticipation that we awaited the arrival of our new chief of mission, a canadian who had been involved in the UN headquarters' pioneer efforts at computerization. We were therefore flabbergasted at his response when some of us proposed that he lead us in converting various systems—the budget and project monitoring systems were the obvious first priorities—to computerized databases.

He brushed aside our suggestion, saying essentially that computers were high-tech tools that were not really appropriate for small-scale field offices. He simply was not interested. So we proceeded on our own to lay the groundwork for an office-wide conversion, and when it was completed, the heretofore disinterested chief of mission crowed about the accomplishment and got credit for it.

Another milestone in my organizational learning curve that says that teamwork often means the top dog does nothing except reap the rewards. I can imagine in some other field offices, where the local staff were more strong-willed and confrontational, that our resident representative, who soon acquired the nickname of non-resident representative due to his frequent out-of-office junkets, would have been reported to the host government and eventually given the heave, but in supine Burma, this was not the favored modus operandi.

Within the spectrum of counterpart government attitudes to foreign assistance programs, Burma could probably be rated somewhere in the middle between a very cooperative host government receptive to UN office ideas, such as Thailand, and a national counterpart that could care less about what the UN thought of its development plans. India fell in the latter category and barely tolerated the presence of foreigners and had no intention of discussing with them how UN funds should be spent.

It was a "take it or leave it" situation: we know what's best for our country, not you foreigners. And they were probably right! There were many well-intentioned Burmese bureaucrats in the government, but the climate of fear in a structure where making a wrong move or a decision that might be at odds with the largely illiterate generals who ran the country created real constraints for us in our work.

A sizcable part of Rangoon's population were ethnic Indians who had been imported by the British in the nineteenth century as heavy laborers, often working in near-slave conditions. These *kala* could be found as wharf workers pulling heavily loaded carts that an animal would have a hard time moving. The luckier ones were employed as *malis* (gardeners), *darawan* (guards), or *dobhi* boys (launderers). A few managed to do quite well as merchants, and a number were employed in our office in clerical positions. But almost all of them remained people without a country. The Burmese refused to give them citizenship, and India had no interest in the grandchild of a laborer who had emigrated from India a hundred years ago.

I recall that one of our best local employees had qualified for a UN job overseas as international staff but was unable to take up the job because he could not get citizenship in either Burma or India. With the ethnic Chinese in Burma, it was an entirely different story. Chinese government policy said that any ethnic Chinese who presented himself at a Chinese embassy would be given immediate citizenship. Thus in addition to its roiling civil war between Shan, Karen, and Burman peoples that had been going on since the British left in 1948, an underbelly of stateless Indians created a wildcard in the Burmese social order that was another potentially serious hindrance to the country's social stability.

Just as His Majesty the King is the lynchpin of strength that holds Thailand together, so Lord Buddha and his religion give Burmese society what cohesion and compassion it manages to have. The network of monasteries and pagodas throughout the country not only provide the population with spiritual strength and guidance in these times of poverty and dictatorship, it also helps to spread what wealth there is so that ordinary citizens can survive. Monasteries often serve as food distribution points and health clinics as well as continuing their traditional role as schools, teaching not only the Buddhist scriptures but also practical subjects, such as English.

I spent many hours visiting temples and pagodas, especially the golden Shwedagon Pagoda, the largest in the country, which was located on a hill near my house. Before I left Burma, I made a sizeable contribution to the Shwedagon, and a memorial plaque bearing my name, both in English and Burmese—my Burmese name being Aung Soe—was installed in the southern wing of the pagoda.

I haven't been back to Burma in nearly twenty years. I'm not sure what I would find if I did return, so I hesitate to go back. Maybe it is better to have fond memories of a place you once loved than to see it again and be disillusioned. Perhaps I will look at my old photo albums and think of the good times and hope that they will return someday.

〖CHAPTER ELEVEN〗

THE LAST RICE FIELD
Memories of Indonesia's Vanishing Rural Life

"When I was in Indonesia, I had a lover, a wonderful man I met on the moving stairs of a department store one rainy afternoon. He was a country boy, a rice farmer who had come to the big city, Jakarta, to seek his fortune. We lived together for nearly four years before I went away to work in another country.

"He was the most beautiful person I had ever met—not just his physical attributes, which were stunning, but what I can only call his purity, his farmer's nobility.

My most memorable moments with him were not lovemaking or holding each other as we gazed shivering at the sea on a foggy day, but jogging together. One afternoon as light fought with oncoming darkness, we ran side by side along a leafy trail near Jakarta's old sports stadium. The rhythm of our gait as we ran was synchronized, and we were so close that our arms brushed each other. I could hear his steady breathing in duet with my own intake of air and smell his sweet sweat; occasionally, I could not resist taking my gaze from the path in front of us and looking into his face. His eyes shone bright, and his smile had that adoring look of new love."

I wrote those words in my diary nearly thirty years ago, shortly after I left Indonesia. Now I am old and live in New York City. As winter approaches and the days grow short, I think of the time I spent with my lover in the tropical Eden that was Indonesia and marvel at how perfect life was for me then. Now shadows here lengthen on the city's gray sidewalks, soon to become treacherous, icy trails; closing my eyes, I remember walking in my lover's village in West Java through the infinite variety of luscious growth in the jungle behind his simple house bathed in tropical sunlight. There were fragrant clove trees and towering coconut palms; the leaves of banana plants would rustle in the breeze with the sound of a hula dancer's grass skirt. Monkeys and owls roosted in the branches of a tall durian grove, screeching and hooting at one another; occasionally, an eagle, the majestic Indonesian garuda, would alight atop the tallest palm, surveilling the realm below him. Nearer to the house, doves hovered in a cage cooing and murmuring in pairs. That is all gone now, I'm told, replaced by concrete and tarmac. The rice fields, too, have disappeared. How do people in Indonesia feed themselves these days, I wonder?

But let's go back to when I was young and the backyard jungle was still a place of mystery and beauty. I know my lover's soul resides in that village. It hovers over me here in my drafty old row house as I stamp my feet and rub my hands to chase away the winter's chill that has settled in my bones.

My first visit to Cilolohan, my lover's village, was back in the early eighties when it was still a small collection of rice farmers' houses surrounded by emerald green paddy fields and lush fruit trees. I was the first foreigner to ever go there, and my arrival was quite an event. First, there were the formalities to dispense with. I had to be registered at what was the equivalent of the mayor's office. Then there was my introduction to his family, which was formal but very friendly. Then I got the surprise of my life. As we sat in the living room of his parents' house, drinking tea, I happened to turn my head around, and there were more than one hundred pairs of eyes, mostly children, who had just come to silently gawk at this *buleh*; they had never seen a real, live Westerner before.

Back then there was little traffic, and the lanes of the village were plied by barefooted villagers, batik-clad women bearing loads of laundry on their heads or children toting buckets of water from the village well. The occasional dolman, a dainty horse-drawn conveyance used to transport passengers or loads of coffee, coconuts, tea, or cloves to market, joined the traffic along with becaks, the local version of the pedicab, with the passengers seated in front of the bicycle-pedaling driver. It was astounding how many passengers and how much cargo could pile into a becak and even more surprising how the driver could make his ponderous load move forward. Like background music to the drama of village life, the constant sound of splashing water could be heard from behind bamboo partitions where baths were being taken before the ever-happening call to prayer.

Cilolohan was only a village, but it had four mosques, and prayers punctuated the rhythm of the inhabitants' existence. They were recited five times a day and were at the heart of life in the village. The *azan* or call to prayer could be heard floating over rooftops and was first sounded at 4:00 a.m. when houses begin to stir for the full morning bath, or *wudlu*. This was followed by half an hour's praying, preferably in the mosque, but if not, on mats at home. It was said in the village that praying in the mosque was *abdol*, more pious, and that these "real" prayers carried more weight where prayers counted, wherever that was. Morning prayers were followed by tea or coffee, and then the whole family would go to the rice fields. Women and men had their separate duties; women planted and harvested, and men plowed the fields, usually with buffalo or sometimes assisted by small tractors. When my lover was a boy, he had a buffalo named Eneng, which means "beautiful woman."

My lover's mother, an independent-minded woman, was not pleased by the humorless, narrow-minded village fanatics who criticized her for not being properly covered and wearing only a tank-top while she worked in the fields. Ignoring village gossip, she also honored the ancient practices of her ancestors with Hindu-Buddhist offerings to the rice gods at harvest time. There was little personal freedom or privacy in rural Indonesia, where tradition tightly regulates almost every move a person makes. Even so, when she died, my lover's mother was mourned by the village for her charitable work in helping the poor. She would make visits to homes of widows and the unemployed, bringing them rice and other food when they were lacking. Returning one afternoon from the rice field twenty-five years ago, she died unexpectedly of a stroke at the age of fifty-five. I remember the first time I met her when I visited their home. She was cooking in the kitchen and looked at me in a shy but friendly way. I saw in her face a farmer's wisdom and the compassion of a mother who had raised thirteen children.

After a couple of hours toil in the paddy fields, the family would return home for breakfast, which usually consisted of rice, fried bananas, tofu, and other side dishes. Then the women would walk to the market for the day's purchases or to sell produce that had been grown at home while the men would go to the garment factories, which were the other main occupation in the village. The factories made school uniforms and other types of clothing, which were sent to the city or even sometimes exported to foreign countries. At noon, families would gather once again at home to pray for half an hour, always ritually bathing before prayer; then they would partake of lunch before returning to the factory or other pursuits. In the case of women, cooking occupied a major part of their day and usually entailed preparing meals for ten to twenty people since families were large and hired help in the fields also had to be fed. In order to cook, firewood had to be gathered, an increasingly difficult task since deforestation had denuded the land of trees. Scavenging for twigs was a chore given to the youngest children of the family.

At 4:00 p.m., the third call to prayer was preceded by a full bath, taking care to observe the ritual gestures for bathing of hands, feet, and face, always avoiding contact with the genitals. Dinner followed and was the main meal of the day; then there was a fourth call to prayer at 6:00 p.m. The fifth and final call to prayer, always preceded by ritual bathing, occurred at 8:00 p.m. By 9:00 p.m., most villagers had retired for the night to rest before facing the next demanding day's workload. On Friday, work was only until 11:00 a.m., after which there was praying in the mosque for two hours. Saturday was a full workday, as was Sunday, except in the case of government offices, which were closed.

In truth, life in the village was more demanding for women than for men. In addition to cooking and farming, women and girls washed laundry on rocks by the river, carrying the heavy loads up and down the banks, and were charged with child care. Often in the dry season, which extended from March to August, women and children were compelled to walk long distances to fetch water from the river or from wells that were full. My lover's mother also ran a madrassa, a religious school that taught Koran reading. She was not a pious person but had inherited the school from her family, and because of her knowledge of Arabic was also a teacher there.

Adult males were charged with siskamling duty, which lasted from 10:00 p.m. until 3:00 a.m. and had been instituted as a security patrol to prevent unlawful acts, mainly robberies, which were carried out by locals or malefactors from other villages. On any given night, as many as ten men were on patrol and would carry bamboo poles or bells, which they would strike ten times once an hour as they walked their rounds. The men would usually pause around 1:00 a.m. for a meal and would cook at the siskamling post, which was a simple bamboo structure on stilts with a fire pit at its base. It was a source of amusement to the village that sometimes the siskamling guards were caught stealing fish from somebody's pond or poaching chickens from a coop to supply their midnight meals. The day after their duty, farmers would usually sleep till noon, but office workers who had been on night guard duty were obliged to go to the office, where they would catch a few snoozes if they could. It was said that everything moved as slow as molasses in the government offices because the bureaucrats were napping off their night guard hangovers.

Life was highly collective in Cilolohan and was governed by the *gotong royong* ethic, a type of mutual, cooperative self-help that extended to building houses, road construction, mosque renovation, well digging, and village clean-ups, to name a few of the tasks that this group effort carried out. Labor was contributed free of charge, with most materials donated. Another group activity popular in Cilolohan and other villages throughout the country was the Arisan, which functioned as a revolving fund for lending money.

Mostly female in membership, the Arisans consisted of as few as ten members who would each contribute an equal amount of money on a monthly basis to create a central fund that was "won" in a lottery held once a month. The winner would then collect the pot and would be thereafter disqualified from the lottery for a set period, until such time as her payments into the fund would recuperate what she had taken out with her lucky draw. The Arisan arrangement was typically Indonesian in its ingenious combination of fun and the luck of the draw while addressing the practical need of providing cash in a society where banking was rare or non-existent.

My lover's grandfather had his own way of saving money. Once a year, he would carve a slot into a long bamboo pole, thus creating a rather elongated, rustic piggy bank. Cash in the form of coins he received for the sale of coconuts would be dropped into the slot, and after twelve months the bamboo pole would be cut open, the coins washed and taken to the local bank in Tasikmalaya and exchanged for paper money, which was then stashed in a secret place in the house. After a couple of years, the money generated from coconut sales would be enough to buy a plot of land for growing rice. After several years' profits from the rice harvest, enough money would have been saved for a haj trip to Mecca, the goal of every villager except my lover's mother. She had no interest in religious pilgrimages.

Then there was the matter of raising horses that became a family story related to my lover by his mother. It appeared that in animal husbandry, human intervention was sometimes needed, as in the case of assisting a male horse to impregnate a mare. My lover's grandfather was adept at such equine manual manipulation, but his grandmother always complained that after such veterinary activity, her husband always wanted to have sex with her! She was very relieved when at a given point he decided to sell all of his horses!

Often on Saturday nights there were entertainments in the form of *wayang golek* puppet shows or *dandut* musical performances or perhaps a *jaipong* singer. Word would circulate from village to village about an upcoming event and, with great anticipation, preparations would be made throughout the preceding week: special food cooked and wrapped in banana leaves, lanterns and bamboo torches to light the path gathered, and *tikar*, the soft woven reed mats so comfortable for sitting, rolled up for the journey. It also happened more than once that after walking two hours to a distant village for an event, it was learned on arrival that the performance had been cancelled or that an idle rumor had been circulated and there never had been any event planned in the first place. Villagers would then laugh, spread their *tikars* on the ground, and have their special dinners without the benefit of the promised cultural offering.

It seemed to matter little whether they were entertained or not. They enjoyed themselves just as much by socializing together and meeting friends from the neighboring village. Unlike Westerners, there were no signs of anger or irritation about missing a performance and no attempt to find the culprit who had spread false information about a promised puppet show. These hardworking, God-fearing villagers were thankful for the simple things in life, and I found their example inspiring.

Life in the village seemed happy, and the level of social harmony was remarkably high, but as a Westerner, I viewed

Cilolohans' social fabric as an intolerably tight weave of control bounded by the mosque and its frequent calls to prayer, the neighbors' ever vigilant eyes and ears ready to comment on any fancied lifestyle infringements, and the constant demands for togetherness in the form of joining an Arisan, participating in *gotong royong* and siskamling activities, and generally being a part of "group think." I remember the story about my lover's sister who had developed an interest in Christianity. Her Catholic schoolmate had invited her to a church Christmas party, but when her mother heard about the invitation and her daughter's plan to attend the service, she locked her in her bedroom the whole day long. Not that his mother cared anything about religion; it was the opinion of the neighbors that counted.

Not long ago, I met my lover in a crowded elevator in a building in New York City—not so different from our first meeting on an escalator years before in Jakarta, I thought. We had not seen each other in twenty-five years. We had both changed, and at first when I saw him, I was not sure it was really the same man. We laughed about how neither of us had hair on our heads anymore and that we had become middle-aged. He told me he had won the green card lottery and had been in New York for several years. I thought how funny it was that huge New York City was really a village where you ran into people just like back in Cilolohan.

I asked him about Cilolohan. How was the jungle behind the house, I wondered. He told me that nothing was the same and that I wouldn't recognize the village anymore. It had become a large town, and three universities had built campuses there and cement parking lots were constructed on what had been rice fields. He said he owned the last rice field in the village; it was the one his mother had worked on the last day of her life. He told me the jungle garden behind his old house had become a housing complex and now everything was concrete and stucco. I asked, "All those beautiful tall trees we used to like are gone?"

He shook his head, laughed, and said, "No, actually there is one tree left. Do you remember the tallest coconut tree that you dared me to climb to pick a coconut for you? It's still there. Somehow it survived the builder's bulldozer and the cement mixer." I shook my head in disbelief and felt tears welling up. I thought I would ask him if he still jogged and if he would like to join me in Central Park some weekend afternoon and maybe we could run together like we used to do in Senayan when we were young lovers. As I dried my eyes with my handkerchief, I looked around the elevator, but he was no longer there. Its doors were closing shut, and I glimpsed his back walking away through the building's crowded lobby. I took a deep breath, choked back a sob, and then smiled to myself, thinking, *New York is just a village like Cilolohan. I know we'll see each other again soon.*

CHAPTER TWELVE

IMPERFECT PARADISE
My Sojourn in the Dragon Kingdom

It was August 1986. I was about to turn forty-seven, and my time in Indonesia was running out. When I say "my time was running out," I hasten to add that I was not doing time in jail or otherwise confined. Quite the contrary, I was as free as one could be and loving my life in a country I now considered to be my home. I had been living in Indonesia, happily settled in a tiny but beautiful home in the garden district of Jakarta, the old Dutch quarter called Menteng. I had met the person who would become my life partner, an

Indonesian from West Java, and we were in the third year of sharing our lives together; and my work with the United Nations was interesting and allowed me to travel the vast and fascinating expanse of the Indonesian archipelago from primitive Irian Jaya to ancient and cultured Java. There was nothing else in life I really needed.

But the time had come when I had serious decisions to make. As a career employee of the United Nations Development Program, I was subject to reassignment according to the "needs of the service." Normally, field assignments outside UN Headquarters in New York were for periods of two to four years. I was about to start my fifth year in Indonesia and had been resisting increasingly insistent requests from our Human Resources Office in New York to accept another assignment somewhere else in the world.

It was axiomatic in the UN that upwardly mobile career officers should not become overly attached to one place or one country. Of course, the UN hastened to add, one should immerse oneself in the country of assignment—learning the local language was encouraged—but one should not under any circumstances go native, which was precisely what was happening to me. I had a circle of friends and a partnership with the person I loved, a local, and, it seemed to me at that moment, that I hadn't the slightest desire to go anywhere else … ever.

My life was perfect. I thought of earlier, perfect moments in my life, such as the time I was scaling the heights of the Matterhorn on a beautiful, clear day, my face bathed by the burning sun, when I said to my companions, "There's no place I'd rather be and nothing else I would rather be doing than being here with you now." Of course, that perfect moment was not to last. Had we stayed much longer on the mountain, the sun would have set and we would have frozen to death. Such is the way of the world. I had had not just one perfect moment in Indonesia, but five perfect years. Why should I end it now?

The problem was breadwinning. If I chose to remain in Indonesia, I would be compelled to separate from the UN where I had been working now for over ten years. I was building a career in a profession—international relations— that I had aspired to since childhood. I felt I was following in my father's footsteps. He had been a successful diplomat who had devoted his professional life to the recovery of Japan after the Second World War, and I had been inspired by his example as I grew up in Japan and saw the results of his tireless efforts. More mundane was the matter of paying my bills and finding steady work. As a generalist, I had no specific, useful skills to market that would land me a job in Indonesia. Developing countries only hired outsiders who had degrees and experience in technical fields like engineering, computer science, and medicine.

The only possibility for me might be to join the staff of one of Jakarta's many English language schools, but even that was problematic. The competition was great since legions of young foreigners, well-qualified in ESL (English as a Second Language) teaching were knocking down the doors of the local language bucket shops, and I had no specific qualification other than native fluency in the language. Even if I were to find an English language teaching position, the pay would be pitiful and it would most likely be part-time.

I would most probably no longer be able to live in my lovely little house with its staff of servants who made life so easy for me. I suppose, had I been a few years younger, I would have thrown caution to the winds and simply done what my heart told me to do, but age was already exercising its influence on the way I did things, and the old adage "We are our parents," was also beginning to influence my thinking.

Imminently practical people, my parents had drilled into me the values of personal responsibility and thinking in a sane manner, doing what was right rather than what the moment told us to do. I may have rebelled against them and what they were trying to instill in me when I was an adolescent, but in recent years, their wisdom had become apparent to me. I also realized that I had become accustomed, thank you, to a diplomat's fat-cat lifestyle with my servants, weekend bungalow in the mountains, and the financial ability to indulge whims like travel and buying nice things for me and my friends. I loved to host dinner parties and pick up the tab at restaurants.

What was I to do? If my personal life and my domestic situation had been normal, my spouse and I would have packed up and moved to Bangkok or Dakar or wherever I had been reassigned to and that would have been that, end of story. But because I was in a same-sex partnership, I had no such option. Living in the shadows in a non-conventional relationship had become my way of life. I had gotten used to it, made accommodations to what society expected of me, and lived happily for the most part, but now I was faced with a situation that threatened to separate me from the one I loved.

I agonized over what I should do with my life. Now I had to deal with what had become the most important decision I would ever have to make. I told my partner, Ari, that if I were to keep my UN job, I would have to leave Indonesia and work in another country. His Javanese equanimity was both comforting and unsettling. Looking at me with his Buddhist face, he simply said, "You'll do what you have to do."

What did that mean? A few days later, Ari left Jakarta and returned to his village in West Java, where he said he had family matters to attend to. Pressure to make the right decision overwhelmed me; the more I thought about what to do, the more confused I became. I was at an impasse. But events would resolve themselves soon enough. When I got home from the office one afternoon, my houseboy ran up to me, saying, "Tuan, a letter has arrived for you from Tasik!" It was the first piece of mail we had ever received and therefore cause for some excitement on the part of Triyono.

I was excited, too, and ripped open the envelope. The letter was from Ari. He said he was going to stay in Tasikmalaya because his family needed him to be there. He told me how much I meant to him and how wonderful our four years together had been for him. He wrote that he hoped it had been good for me, too. He wished me luck and told me he hoped we could meet again one day. I read and reread his letter many times and realized he had made my decision for me.

Where would I go? Which part of the world would I be sent to? I thought I would like to go to a remote place, a hardship assignment, an exotic locale where I could forget for a time what I was going through. I had recently been offered an assignment and a promotion if I went to Guyana, an English-speaking country on the northern coast of Latin American. Most of its inhabitants were descendants of indentured Asian Indians who had been sent there to work the plantations when the country was a British colony.

Its politics were interesting, being governed by the Marxist, Chedi Jagan. Working there would indeed be an adventure. I was tempted but still held out for something better. The UN encouraged its career staff to work in as many different regions of the world as possible, but I preferred to stay in Asia. I had grown up in Japan and had already worked for many years in Southeast Asia—Vietnam, Thailand, Burma, and Indonesia—and I felt drawn, if not addicted, to that part of the world.

The French had a phrase for it, *le mal jaune* or yellow fever, which described white Westerners who could never leave the Asian tropics. Pushing my luck, I asked my headquarters to find me another assignment in Asia. Placement would not be as easy for me as it had been for earlier postings since I had reached a senior level in the organizational hierarchy where there were fewer options. I waited to see what the powers in headquarters would offer me, half-expecting to be given Africa on a take-it-or-leave-it basis.

I was surprised when I was asked if I might be interested in going to the Himalayan Kingdom of Bhutan. I immediately accepted their offer. Bhutan seemed to be just the kind of place I needed. I could throw myself into my job and be diverted by the newness of an environment that was totally strange to me. And my yellow fever addiction would still be satisfied even though where I was headed would not be in the tropics.

Detailed planning had never been my strong suit. I threw what I owned into a couple of suitcases and, with the help of my houseboy and cook, packed the rest of my belongings into crates that were to be sent via sea and mountain road up to Thimphu, the capitol of Bhutan. My most prized possessions were family photographs and a ceramic jar that Ari had brought for me from his village, a very unique piece of pottery that had been carved from clay rather than being made on a pottery wheel. I had never seen anything as rustic and beautiful.

I also had numerous lengths of batik, the fabled cloth of Java whose tones and fanciful designs were a joy to touch, wear, or look at. I hoped that these few belongings would arrive at their new home in one piece. The moving company who packed my personal effects assured me that everything would arrive in ship-shape condition. Promises, promises! It was not to be. While I realized where I was going was not tropical, I made no efforts to supplement my light-weight Jakarta wardrobe with heavier clothing that would be needed at altitudes of nearly ten thousand feet.

This oversight would later prove to be one of many problems I would encounter in my new assignment, but by no means the worst. The biggest challenges I would face would have nothing to do with planning or even putting my nose to the grindstone and working hard. As my time in Indonesia grew shorter with the days shrinking into hours, I compiled a scrapbook of photos and wrote an accompanying text narrating the good times Ari and I had shared together. I put it in the mail and hoped it would reach him.

In those days, the eighties, getting to Bhutan was no easy job. Until not that long ago, travel to the interior was done by caravan and took days, and although there were now air connections to Paro, a valley town several hours drive from the Bhutanese capital, the trip had to be made via Calcutta, where one waited sometimes days for the tiny plane that would deliver passengers to the Dragon Kingdom.

I arrived in crumbling, crowded, chaotic Calcutta from Bangkok. The stark contrast between Thailand's glittering metropolis and its jet-set, state-of-the art international airport and what I found on arrival at Dum Dum, the aerodrome in Bengal, was almost beyond description. Making my way through the teeming depot suffused with the blended odors of *pan* (betel nut) and astringent latrine cleanser, my first misstep was to have a head-on collision with the luggage cart of a memsahib, an Englishwoman who was also travelling to Bhutan.

She shrieked in disbelief as our Samsonites collided, and as we unlocked our bruised conveyances, we apologized profusely to each other. Later we would meet in Thimphu and developed a lively rapport, which would turn into a close friendship that I still cherish today. One thing can be said for travel. It takes the mind off of things past; sad thoughts and memories are shoved into the background, especially when one is locked in a battle for the survival of the fittest that is the usual state of play in Indian airports.

Cities are like people. You either love them or hate them without knowing exactly why. I loved Calcutta from the moment I entered it. Surcharged with atmosphere is the best way I can describe why I developed an instant love affair with this crumbling, colonial slum. Perhaps another way of describing Calcutta is "not boring." And I was grateful to this grand, rather pathetic place for diverting me when I most needed distraction.

I don't remember how long I stayed in Calcutta this first of many visits, but I found myself one morning seated in a mosquito of an airplane, being sucked and blown about by mountain valley currents as we navigated our way into a nose dive to Paro, the mountain valley airport town that was the air traveler's point of entry into Bhutan. The plane skimmed rooftops laden with large, red, drying chili peppers, and tall, tattered prayer flags flapped in the wind. I realized I was coming to a very different place.

My first impression of Bhutan was that of deep, pleasantly booming voices. Bhutanese speech is delivered in exactly the opposite way from the American manner of speaking. The latter produces sounds that are essentially nasal and a bit whiny, whereas the sound of Bhutan is rich and full-bodied, coming from deep down in the diaphragm, the *oom-oom* chanting place, and is not unlike a fragrant, warm tot of good Jamaican rum. And being near a Bhutanese when he speaks is also a unique experience.

Dressed in their traditional garb, the homespun, kimonolike kho, most Bhutanese produce an interesting personal odor, a fusion of betel nut, which they chew incessantly, combined with more than a whiff of stale unwashed body perfume, which blended together, when one gets used to it, results in a rather atmospheric, seductive package. I later learned that the consumption of betel nut was to be approached with caution.

I had on occasion nibbled on it in other countries that had the habit—Burma and Thailand—but the variety favored in Bhutan was strictly for pros. Once during an appointment with a betel-chewing government official, I was proffered the nut, which I consumed with gusto, only to be seized moments later with waves of drenching perspiration and a giddy feeling that could be classified as a major trip. Think of a thousand cups of Starbucks espresso packed into one tiny cup, topped off with a Dexedrine tablet!

The Bhutanese are extraordinarily handsome people. The native Drukpa possess features that are essentially Tibetan in character: high cheek bones and strong facial sculpture, which is softened by constant smiling and laughter. In isolated rural mountain areas, more than a few of the natives have cleft palates, and prematurely gray hair is also frequently seen. Perhaps these unusual traits result from the inbreeding that has transpired over the centuries.

Otherwise beautiful faces are sometimes marred by hideous scars resulting from bear attacks that occur even near the larger towns. Mingled with the Drukpa people are ethnic Indians and Nepalese. Many of the latter have become Bhutanese citizens, and most of them live in southern Bhutan in the tropical Terai area.

My first home in Bhutan was the Hotel Druk, located in what passed as Thimphu's main drag, a sorry little street where vehicles drove around old ladies who might suddenly squat in the middle of the road to pee. A modest accommodation, it was where I was to live for several months until permanent housing became available.

A recent spike in the non-Bhutanese population due to an increase in foreign aid and technical assistance from first-world governments and development organizations, and the concomitant arrival of new legions of the development set, had created a housing shortage in the capital, and I was compelled to join the queue until something came on the market.

My first night in Thimphu, I was on my own and beginning to feel lonely. The diversion and bustle of Calcutta was not there to keep me amused, and I found myself thinking of my beautiful partner whom I had left back in Indonesia. It was then that I began to think I had been a fool to leave him and the country I had come to love. Who cared about making lots of money and occupying a lofty position when there was nobody to come home to at night? As I sat in my room in the gathering gloom of an afternoon already turning dark, I found myself on the verge of tears.

What would surely have turned into a crying jag was suddenly averted by a knock on my door. I opened it to meet my new boss and his wife and daughter for the first time. John Sloan-Williams was a pleasant-looking Englishman about my own age. He was accompanied by his wife, Seema, a statuesque, well-born Indian woman who had a striking resemblance to the folk singer Joan Baez. Their eleven-year-old daughter smiled and offered me a box of welcome cookies she had baked.

We spoke easily with each other, and I found myself taking an immediate liking to them. Unlike most Brits in international service, he was not the colonel blimp know-it-all or the more insidious patronizing type of Englishman who constantly murmured his concern for the less fortunate of the world. Elegant in speech and gentle in manner, I came to know Sloan-Williams as a tough-minded but always fair development professional who seemed genuinely dedicated to his nation-building mission.

We parted company and agreed to meet the next morning at the office for my introduction to the staff. I sat in my room and reflected on the good fortune that had landed me in an assignment with what seemed to be a good boss. I had had some less-than-stellar supervisors in previous assignments, and it was especially heartening to know that in a small, isolated duty station, the person I would often rub elbows with was a decent sort. I descended to the hotel dining room for an evening meal, not so much because I was hungry but due to my nagging loneliness. As I sat alone in the stuffy little restaurant eating lukewarm Brown Windsor soup and drinking flat beer, I wondered why Sloan-Williams had not invited me to his home for a welcome dinner my first solitary night in Bhutan. I knew I would never understand the dos and don'ts and nuances of protocol.

My debut at the office the following day was an eye-opener for me in terms of where I now was in the bureaucratic pecking order. As a deputy, I was second in command in a rather sizeable office, not just another officer. When the resident representative was out of the country I was the AI or ad interim, carrying the temporary rank of chief of mission or ambassador, with the right to fly the UN flag on my chauffeur-driven vehicle. Heady stuff!

As I met the staff with whom I was to work and supervise during the course of my assignment in Bhutan, I experienced a new sensation, being deferred to by people who otherwise would have treated me as an equal and a colleague. The sensation was a bit unsettling, and I hoped I would handle my new elevated status in the right way.

Sloan-Williams offered me the key to the executive washroom adjoining his office. I thanked him but never used it. Even though the "common" staff latrine was dank and a bit smelly, and I would have preferred the more luxurious facilities, I felt that by using them, I might become indebted to my new boss. I also thought the staff would somehow respect me more if I did not elevate myself in this rather petty way. As I was to learn soon enough, such token acts of false modesty as using the common loo would get me nowhere when the office environment became hostile.

In the months to come I would get to know the staff as we worked together; I faced the challenge of managing a diverse team that consisted of strong players as well as weak links. Juggling the varying abilities of each person to the benefit of the organization and the country we were serving was not always an easy task. There were two outstanding young officers, one European and one North American. I could trust them with anything and heaped increasing quantities of work on their desks without hearing a complaint or seeing a dip in the quality of their performance.

Other staff were more problematic. A beautiful, young South Asian woman named Indra, an Angelina Jolie lookalike, had joined the office recently as international staff. She had been educated at an elite American graduate school and possessed that almost indescribable quality I call star power. When she entered a room, all heads turned, and her speech was captivating, a mesmerizing blending of Indian and upper-class English accents. Just watching her smoke a cigarette sent chills up my spine.

I was briefed by my boss, who said my predecessor had found her useless and had recommended that her contract not be renewed when the first year had been completed. With performance reviews coming up soon, he told me that her fate was in my hands. Although I grew to like her tremendously and realized that I was totally enthralled by her, I had to agree that my predecessor was right. Her work performance was "all hat and no cattle," to borrow a Texas expression for zero value. But Indra was clever and manipulative, a consummate politician who had cultivated senior Bhutanese government officials.

More complicated, she had charmed me so totally that I was caught in her thrall and could not bring myself to

give her the ax. When the time came to evaluate her performance, I made the decision to recommend a renewal of
her contract although I never trusted her with serious work.
Such are the compromises and maneuvers of a diplomat, especially a queer one! More to the point and a testament to
my own lack of professionalism, this craven posture I had
taken demonstrated that even a gay man is vulnerable to the
fatal spell of female charm!

Another personnel challenge came in the form of a towering six-foot-five Dutchman named Win de Jong. Win was
amiability personified. The problem was he was drunk from
the time he arrived at the office each morning. His sponsor, the Netherlands, was an influential country whose deep
pockets had resulted in generous grants for the development
of Bhutan. We decided it would not be desirable to give
Win the boot and resolved ourselves to have him staggering
around the office for another year or so.

Thus for various reasons, I felt compelled to go light on
a number of staff members who, under ordinary conditions,
should have been gotten rid of. My nemesis turned out to be
a fellow American, Robert McCall. His wicked work would
cause me no end of trouble and be one of the causes for my
early departure from Bhutan.

Bhutan was a monarchy, not yet a constitutional one,
ruled by a king, but the real power in the kingdom was
India, which had established a network of military posts
throughout the country and held economic and financial pre-
dominance over its commercial life. Fortunately for Bhutan,
it had joined the United Nations some years earlier, thereby
avoiding the fate of Sikkim, a small Himalayan kingdom
that had been annexed by India in the seventies.

The Bhutanese were predominantly small-scale subsistence farmers. Other occupations included the military and government service; unlike most developing countries, civil servants in Bhutan were very well-paid, and unemployment was almost non-existent. This made it difficult for us to recruit qualified local staff for our office. The shortage of labor in the construction and services sectors resulted in the importation of large numbers of Indian guest workers to work in such menial tasks as road construction and garbage collection. The country would not have functioned without these miserably paid, poorly treated foreigners.

Eventually I found a pleasant house and eagerly awaited my household goods, which were reported to be travelling by truck along the bumpy, mountain road to Thimphu. Three months of hotel food and a cramped little room were getting on my nerves, and I looked forward to sitting in my own living room and doing a bit of gardening in the backyard. The gap in my life was the absence of Ari, my partner. We decided that he should join me in Bhutan. His skill and experience as a clothing designer and garment factory manager could probably qualify him for work in the Bhutanese Handicraft Emporium, which was hoping to turn Bhutan's beautiful local textiles into stylish clothing for export.

He had been offered a job there as a design consultant, and I was beside myself when I thought of being with him again. Bhutan was nice enough, but it had been a very lonely place for me. Now all that would change, I hoped. Since the status of our partnership could not be recognized by the UN and Bhutan, we were compelled to arrange a costly tourist visitor's visa that might be renewed by making under-the-table payments to the right people. We both found these arrangements distasteful and demeaning, but we had no alternative.

I had planned to go to Calcutta to meet Ari and hoped our household goods would arrive before he did so I could welcome him to our new home in style, furnished with items familiar to both of us. It was with no small amount of anticipation and excitement that I rushed to our office one Monday morning to receive my shipment, which had arrived the previous evening. But apparently the crates had not been packed as carefully as the Jakarta shipper had promised. When I reached the office compound, I was crushed and saddened to see my crates smashed and broken to bits, laying in the muddy driveway. The delivery truck had just dumped the broken crates onto the ground in front of my office and left.

My belongings were scattered every which way; the glass frame on my mother's beautiful photograph had been broken, and the treasured ceramic urn from Ari was scattered and smashed to bits. The office staff watched me in silence as I knelt to pick up its pieces. From this point on, my life in Bhutan went into a downward spiral in spite of Ari's comforting presence.

Ari and I settled into our house, which was nicely located on a hill overlooking town. Next to us was a Buddhist pagoda, whose bells and gongs provided sweet music of an evening. With seeds we had brought in from France, we planted a garden and soon had a wide variety of vegetables that, together with Ari's genius in the kitchen, made meals at our house a sought-after invitation. The world outside of our house was not so friendly. I found that we were excluded from dinners and most other social functions that constituted the Thimphu social whirl, and several government officials, including the foreign minister, had turned their back to me when I had approached them at a reception.

I began to feel increasingly marginalized in this very small town of traditional values. I wondered why the UN had ever consented to the assignment of a gay man to a tiny duty station where his lifestyle, as quiet and sedate as it was, would have been a point of controversy and cause for his being ostracized and rejected.

In my previous assignments, I had been highly popular and successful in my dealings with UN colleagues as well as government officials. But these earlier postings had been in large cities, and I was able to conceal my homosexuality, whereas in tiny Thimphu, a town of twenty thousand, nobody could take a leak without the whole community knowing about it.

The nail in my coffin came about as a result of a conflict in the office that arose when I warned the American McCall and his Bhutanese assistant about their non-attendance at staff meetings. I told them that such a disregard of office procedure was unacceptable and that their continued insubordination would be reflected in their performance reports. Their sullen response left me convinced that they were unrepentant. As I was to learn, that was an understatement.

A month later, Sloan-Williams called me into his office and showed me a letter from our director in New York headquarters. The letter detailed actions that had been taken by McCall and his colleague who had reported to headquarters that I had AIDS, that I was spreading the disease to others, and that I should be deported immediately from Bhutan. Sloan-Williams acted admirably. He arranged for McCall's immediate departure from Bhutan and reassured me that I should carry on with my work and life as though nothing had happened. But the damage had been done as far as I was concerned.

I felt I had been marginalized and could no longer function effectively in my position. I also began to fear for my personal safety. One day my Nepali houseboy burst into my office, sobbing, his face a river of blood. He had been beaten up by a Bhutanese for no good reason. Would I be next? Some months before, I had undergone a medical examination in Singapore, and it was discovered that I had a heart murmur and hypertension. I communicated with our headquarters, asking for early departure from Bhutan and reassignment on medical grounds. The request was granted, and I was directed to report to the neighboring country of Dhaka, Bangladesh, for my new assignment.

My departure from Bhutan was a far cry from my arrival. There was no farewell dinner and no chauffeur-driven sedan to take us to the airport. The office sent a beaten-up old VW van to the house, and we rode in it along with other passengers to the airport in Paro. Sloan-Williams did manage to make an appearance at our house minutes before the van departed. We shook hands, and that was it. I was told that he had elaborately feted my predecessor on the eve of his departure. Zip for me. With what had transpired during the past year and a half, I saw my bright UN career going up in smoke. The professional purgatory of the coming months would confirm my feeling. As Ari and I flew out on the mosquito plane to Calcutta, I reflected on our time in Bhutan and what it all had meant.

I tried to focus on the happy moments and the beautiful things we had experienced: the people, the scenery, the serene Buddhism. My successor and his wife had arrived before my departure, and I hoped they would have a better experience than I had had. Apparently, they did. I ran into him some years later when we both had been reassigned back to New York headquarters, and he raved about his four years in the paradise of the Dragon Kingdom. He told me the garden Ari and I had planted in the backyard of our house on the hill in Thimphu was still flourishing and the new inhabitants of the house were enjoying it. I smiled and thought to myself, *At least we did one thing right.*

[CHAPTER THIRTEEN]

GOATS WALTZING ON THE BALLROOM FLOOR
A Bengali Interlude

Bangladesh is one of the world's best-kept secrets. Invariably maligned by the Western press since its stormy inception as a break-away state from distant Pakistan in the early seventies—the utter folly of its ever being part of that faraway place makes the head spin—East Bengal has been described as an international basket case synonymous with natural disaster, corruption, political chaos, and famine. First-world pundits have flogged this third-world whipping post relentlessly in spite of good news stories that could have been written; one especially comes to mind: Muhammad Yunus winning the Nobel Prize for his innovative work in micro-financing by way of the Grameen Bank.

That's the big picture. Let's get down to where the tire meets the road or where the buffalo plows the rice paddy and talk about a place that I know: the country I found to be one of the nicest spots on earth. Bangladesh's rich culture, its physical beauty, the grace and intelligence of its people and last but not least, its cloyless cuisine, should make it a rival to places like Thailand for the tourist trade, but nary a traveler visits Bangladesh for pleasure. One wonders why this is, why it has not been discovered, and once again, the finger has to be pointed at the media, which, like a bad Broadway review, can make or break the reputation of a country with the stroke of a pen.

I first came to know Bangladesh by sheer chance. It was a roll of the dice that sent me there in 1988 for what was supposed to be an interim assignment with the United Nations. For a variety for reasons, my assignment in neighboring Bhutan had been curtailed before the normal reassignment date, and UN Headquarters was at a loss as to what to do with me. After being in a holding pattern for what seemed like an eternity, a phone call from the Human Resources Office in New York reached me in Bhutan, and they suggested I might want to go to Bangladesh as a program advisor, a nebulous title that seemed to mean everything and nothing.

Years before, when I was working in Thailand, I had heard good things about Bangladesh from a colleague whose opinion and taste I respected. When the personnel puppeteer in headquarters suggested that I might like to "think it over for a few days," I surprised her with an immediate acceptance and within a short time was on my way to Dhaka.

Camping for months in a hotel seemed to be my fate whenever I took up an assignment in a new country. It had been the case in Burma, Indonesia, and Bhutan. Now once again I found myself making my home in temporary quarters; this time it was the Dhaka Hilton. At least it wasn't like the seedy Soviet-style Inya Lake Hotel in Rangoon where brainwashed North Koreans marched robotlike into the dining room promptly at six o'clock every night, or the musty Hotel Druk in Thimphu, with its damp sheets and odor of curry clinging to the walls.

Compared to those two unfortunate hostelries, it was a luxurious paradise, but therein lay the problem. Next to the hotel was a gigantic garbage dump, which was inhabited by scavengers, many of them small children barely old enough to walk. Clinging to the chain link fence separating them from the Hilton's luxurious precincts, they would stare silently as the hotel's well-heeled guests sipped cocktails in the well-tended garden or went for another set of tennis

Try as I would to ignore this depressing scene, it would eat away at me while I dined and followed me about like a bad dream. I wanted to slap the spoiled, overfed expat brats in the hotel dining room and drag them to the chain link fence to show them what life in the real world was about. In many other developing countries, it was not hard to forget about poverty and misfortune. Swaying palms and Buddhists temples tended to pull the eye away from harsh reality. It somehow always seemed more out of sight. Not in Bangladesh. The grim reaper was always there with his hand held out, reminding you of the hideous gap between the world's haves and those who had nothing.

I had found the place I wanted to live in, but it would not be available for another few months, so I resigned myself to hotel food and life in a lobby until I could settle in the beautiful apartment in Dammondi that would be my home for the next two years. The contrast with Thimphu, the capital of Bhutan, was striking. The population of Dhaka numbered in the millions while Thimphu was a village of twenty thousand. Even so, I managed to end up living in a beautiful, green neighborhood not favored by the foreign community because it had no Western amenities, like supermarkets.

It did have lakes and gorgeous flame trees that bloomed gloriously in the hot season preceding the monsoon. There was also a mosque nearby whose soothing call to prayer would reach me on my verandah of an evening. Another neighbor was the Soviet Cultural Center, where one could sample the offerings of this Communist paradise. It was especially interesting to visit the Soviet Cultural Center as the USSR slipped inexorably into decline. It seemed the closer it got to collapse, the more grandiose its cultural displays became.

My office was within easy walking distance of where I lived, and I was content to take the fifteen-minute stroll to the UN every morning until I discovered the Bengali pedicab, that quaint rickshaw conveyance propelled by manpower from a modified bicycle mounted in front of the passenger's seat. My routine became set. I would have breakfast, and my housekeeper, Abdul, would go out to the street to flag down a rickshaw driver who would be waiting for me by the time I came out of the house.

I enjoyed my rickshaw rides and found it one of the small ways I could become a bit more local, a bit native, just as wearing the *longyi* or sarong had made me a little bit Burmese when I lived in Rangoon. But my rickshaw-riding days were to be short-lived. One morning when we were passing a quiet, tree-lined area with no traffic or pedestrians, our rickshaw was accosted by a motorcycle ridden by three young men. The bike screeched to a halt in front of the rickshaw, and two of the riders leaped off and lunged at us. One of them brandished an implement resembling a letter opener and grabbed my briefcase.

He examined its contents and, finding only UN documents inside, flung the satchel with disgust into a nearby field where goats had been pastured. The papers flew about every which way, and the briefcase landed in a water hole. Wasting no time, the four-footed creatures devoured the UN reports and my briefcase. I hope they enjoyed their meal and are all the wiser for the weighty matters they consumed.

I found the office scene in Dhaka one more instance of same-old, same-old. I was beginning to think that developing countries did not need a heavy foreign presence with expatriate "experts" telling locals how to run their lives and their country. Without question, countries like Bangladesh did need assistance with their problems, but the form that assistance often took made me think that the donors were benefitting more than the recipients.

In the case of the UN, projects were relatively small and, in my opinion, overstaffed by highly paid foreigners. It would have been better to consolidate various budgets and attack a really big problem, like flood control, with massive assistance that would address the country's most serious problem: floods and the menace of rising water levels, which, with global warming, could inundate one-quarter of the country in the not-too-distant future. The Dutch, experts in that field, stood ready to offer the technical advice, but funding never seemed to materialize. Too many vested interests kept finances and their protected programs fragmented.

I was a bit taken aback to run into my old colleague and boss from Burma, who had surfaced as chief of mission in the Dhaka office, the so-called non-resident representative, the canadian computer expert who had shown no interest in leading our Rangoon office into the computer age at the beginning of the eighties. If anything, time had made him even more detached in attitude and less involved in the program he was overseeing in Bangladesh.

The show was run by an ambitious Belgian, amorously involved with a young woman who was a program officer in my section. Because of their liaison and her perception of the power structure in the office, she seemed to feel immune to any supervisory role I might want to exercise in the execution of her official duties. Soon I was to realize that word had gotten around the office that I was a bird of flight who had landed in their midst and who had no future in that office. I was a "day-tripper" who was expected to be reassigned before too long. The determining bottom line in most organizations is power, and it was obvious that I possessed little of this potent commodity.

I felt the UN Dhaka office was grossly overstaffed with internationals, who each had their portfolio of projects, which they were charged with monitoring and evaluating. Total "make-work," in my opinion. Once a week, we were summoned around a long conference table for a morning of show-and-tell to report on how our projects were doing. At these meetings, I usually sat next to a married couple, an older Dutchman and his younger Italian wife. She was in charge of a number of agricultural projects while he looked after the industrial sector. Their invariable opening line at these meetings was to announce that "Agriculture and Industry are present and accounted for."

Usually positioned next to this couple was an emaciated Pakistani, brilliantly articulate and of hideous mien. As we sat down for the meetings, he would invariably smirk at me and say in his impeccable BBC accent, "On top of our projects, are we?" knowing that I had just arrived and was still familiarizing myself with my portfolio. To his left was a young Japanese officer who had recently graduated from Yale and who had acquired that unfortunate American body language tick that involved raising his hands to the level of his face and wiggling the index and middle fingers of both hands to indicate quotation marks. The constant use of these manual inverted commas gave him the appearance of wanting to take off and fly when he spoke.

I came to dread these weekly gatherings and did everything in my power to avoid them. The best way out was to visit projects in the countryside outside Dhaka, and I took advantage of such trips as often as possible. In so doing, I discovered a country rich in beauty and culture and a people seriously dedicated to their own self-improvement. The so-called NGO/PVO (non-governmental organization/ private voluntary organization) scene in Bangladesh was the most fertile and innovative engine for development I had ever seen. Most of these organizations were local. I became increasingly convinced that Bangladeshis could meet their country's challenges with less foreign involvement. While foreign financial assistance and a minimum of well-placed advisory services were needed, I felt that the excess of expats in the country resulted in people stepping on each other's feet as well as actually causing harm in some cases.

One example was particularly telling. Foreign assistance programs had been giving high priority to the health sector and focused on such activities as training of nurses. I was therefore flabbergasted when our non-resident representative called a meeting one afternoon and introduced an American businessman to us, saying the entrepreneur had come with a very important proposal to help Bangladesh. It appeared that this middleman functioned as a broker, recruiting Bangladeshi doctors and nurses for work in short-staffed American hospitals. I found myself drawing a blank, wondering how such an enterprise could possibly help Bangladesh, which was desperately short of medical personnel and was spending annually a large chunk of its budget to close this gap.

What was the point in using scarce resources to train much needed personnel and then shipping them overseas to developed countries like the United States? I suppose in his own convoluted way, the businessman was correct in what he said, and that his hiring away nurses to go to the States would help increase Bangladesh's foreign remittances by the money these people would send home to their families. But how would this actually help the country? There would certainly be more motorcycles and cell phones, but what about the quality of health care?

The particularly worrisome aspect of this scheme was that it was especially attractive to young graduates, who could earn in a month in the United States what they would earn in a year in their home country. And we, the UN, were being asked to aid and abet this damaging mission. I was shocked when our non-resident representative dithered and murmured about what a good thing it would be!

It was common knowledge that corruption was rampant in Bangladesh, and I got a first-hand look at what was happening when I befriended a young local named Hussein. We met through a mutual American friend who had done business in the country some years earlier and who told me about the invaluable role played by "expeditors," those people who influenced which foreign company would win a contract and how the budgets funding the foreign presence would be handled once the projects got rolling.

Hussein was a charming guy and became a good friend, helping me experience the real Bangladesh through visits to his family farm and his own home, where his gracious mother presided over meals to which I was invited. But it became soon apparent to me that the likes of Hussein and the system he thrived on were costing foreign donors and the masses of poor Bangladeshis a huge chunk of the resources that should have gone to the people. Add to this outright waste, in the form of bribes and palm-greasing, the sad reality of botched projects and ineptly executed activities, and I would estimate that less than one-third of the money destined for projects ever found its way to the rightful destination. While I was by no means a Maoist, I began to think that the chairman's policy of tough-minded self-reliance was perhaps the best approach.

I began spending more time exploring the obscure neighborhoods of Dhaka, which held a treasure of colonial and pre-colonial architecture. Stately buildings revealed to me that Dhaka had not been the backwater I had assumed it was during the pre-independence period. I was particularly taken by what I found along the city's waterfront. I had befriended a Bengali professor who was also an adviser to several of our UNESCO projects and, with my encouragement, Dr. Nasimuddin Ahmed organized weekend excursions to little-known quarters of the city

One Sunday he led a group of us to the riverbank into one of poorest sections of town I had ever seen. Alleys teemed with life, and I realized the hundreds of people I saw were actually living on the street, their few worldly possessions piled on the sidewalk. Dr. Ahmed led us through a narrow maze, stepping over cooking fires and families sitting on mats eating rice with their fingers from banana leaves, and up a dark passage of creaking stairs.

After a shaky ascent, we suddenly found ourselves in a huge room bathed by the afternoon sun. Looking out a large window over the river dappled by golden rays of light, I heard Dr. Ahmed explain that we were in the largest of the old *nawab* or princely palaces and that we were in the ballroom. Standing on a marble floor, I looked around me and overhead saw a ceiling painted in a vast Poussin-esque fresco of blue sky, puffy clouds, and flying angels. Gilded columns lined walls now cracked and stained with age.

In the corner was a woman in rags with two goats. She was milking one of them while a fire burned from a kerosene stove, warming parboiled rice. She was one of Dhaka's many squatters. Seeing us, she touched her forehead in an ancient gesture of fealty and subservience to superiors and held out her other hand, hoping for alms. The whole scene took my breath away. I could imagine, less than half a century before, uniformed lords and bejeweled ladies of the realm swaying to Strauss waltzes, assured their comfortable empire would go on forever. Now the room was empty except for the goat lady; the floor's marble was dulled by the dust of ages and only ghosts danced to the bleat of a goat with swollen teats.

A few days later, I had the rare chance to visit the Bangladeshi Parliament building, one of the triumphs of modern architecture designed by the noted American architect Louis Kahn, who had died of a heart attack in a stall of the men's room in New York City's Penn Station. Constructed in unfinished concrete, set on an artificial lake, the building was a stunning series of flying pavilions that included not only legislative chambers but also living quarters for families of the members of Parliament. Through the kindness of my friend the fixer, Hussein, we were being entertained by the wife and children of one of the members of Parliament. Later, the member of Parliament joined us and spoke of his hopes for the future and for Bangladesh.

That afternoon, I returned to my apartment and sat on the verandah, looking out at the blazing flame trees and the mosque's white spire. My housekeeper brought me my usual early evening gin and tonic, and I thought about this country, teeming with people and an ancient culture that had managed to survive the ravages of poverty and the onslaught of globalized homogenization. I had faith that Bangladesh would somehow make it, in spite of the surfeit of foreign meddling and the perverse forces of nature that lashed its shores and ravaged its fields. I recalled a banner I had seen in the Parliament building that said, *"Bangladesh Zindabad!"* Long live Bangladesh!

[CHAPTER FOURTEEN]

DON'T QUIT YOUR REGULAR JOB!
A Would-Be Singer's Rocky Road to Nowhere

It started like this. I had a dream. And in that dream I was standing on a stage, bathed in lights, gentle rose-colored rays trained on my face. Through this gauzy illumination, I saw an audience. I had just finished a song, probably a cabaret ballad by Stephen Sondheim, most likely "Send in the Clowns." There was thunderous applause; with slightly parted lips on their faces, my fans registered that expression of awe and wonderment that all performers crave. I bowed slightly and cleared my throat for the next selection. It was that fifties' hit song from *Pajama Game* called "Hey There." Eddie Fisher had taken it to the top of the charts. I slid into the lyrics, the velvet tones of my lounge singer's voice caressing the words.

The audience remained captivated. Even that busy lady talking non-stop suddenly stopped her chatter, looked up at me adoringly and gripped her rolled up program in her diamond-studded hands. I knew at the end of the set that she would want my autograph.

Actually my dream was a daydream, and I was standing in the shower at the YMCA singing my heart out. I thought I was the only person in the shower, but while I was taking my curtain call, someone else had sneaked in, and while he was soaping up, he listened to me! Should I stop my lullaby or continue? I compromised by lowering my voice, melting the words into a hum. When I finished, my showermate looked at me and said, "You know, that song means a lot to me because I was in the Broadway musical and the movie of *Pajama Game*. I'm the guy who played the labor union rep, and I sang '7 ½ Cents!'"

Wow! I was dumbstruck. Another one of those only-in-New-York-City experiences. Two weeks before I had seen Woody Allen in Central Park, and the week before that, Elaine Stritch and I had played tug-of-war at a deli door on Seventh Ave. And now I was actually talking to a show biz celebrity. As he was leaving the shower, my new acquaintance told me he knew of a good voice teacher if I was interested. He suggested I might want to take some lessons.

Did this mean he thought I was promising or just really bad? I had never sung before, let alone had a voice lesson, but I thought, *What the hell! It might be fun!* I had just received a sum of money from my employer, having recently retired, and we retirees were given some funds to take lessons in any subject of our choice so that our leisure years would be productive and we wouldn't go off and become alcoholics or slip into depression and kill ourselves. Some of my colleagues had taken cooking classes; another had gone back to school to learn how to start a small business selling orchids. I hadn't tapped my grant yet and the window of time for using it was about to expire. Why not blow it on voice lessons? At least I couldn't hurt myself!

Later in the locker room, my new shower friend introduced himself. He was Jack Straw, and he gave me the name of his friend who was a voice teacher. Her name was Ann Tell. Some days later, I rang Ann and asked if she was free to take on another student. She said she was, and I made my way to a building just north of Times Square, in the theater district. She lived in the tiniest apartment I had ever seen. It couldn't have been any larger than 250 or 300 square feet, but it accommodated a big, white upright piano. I was on my way!

Ann was an open-faced, friendly lady somewhere in her late seventies, although she was the type of person you don't pin an age to. She was just Ann. Amiable, always smiling and laughing, full of energy. She had grown up on a farm in Iowa and, bitten by the show business bug, had come to New York City in the late thirties. Her own voice was a mellow alto, and her specialty was, interestingly, singing Hawaiian songs.

She had lots of stories to tell that painted an atmospheric picture of what it had been like being young, talented, and a newcomer to the city back when New York was gritty, glitzy Gotham. She recounted how in 1940, she and a group of Hawaiian singers and dancers had been entertaining on a cruise liner bound for Argentina, and near Buenos Aires, the ship had been stopped by a German navy destroyer and they were held overnight by the Nazi navy. Perfect officers and gentlemen, those Nazis , Ann said. She also told me that she had been in a contest with Dinah Shore that launched Shore's career and that she, Ann, would have won had she been a blonde at that time.

Over the course of a couple of years in my weekly voice lessons with Ann, I got a pretty good idea of what kind of talent I had and realized it was pretty modest at best. New York City is full of voice teachers; they are a dime a dozen, and most of them are desperately in need of income and clients. None of them are going to tell you that you are a talent-free disaster and that you should pursue another hobby. They keep encouraging you, and you keep coming back. "Now let's have another warm-up, go through those scales one more time … are you ready for your song now? And don't forget your phrasing." Ann was very supportive, but in her case I felt she really thought I could make a singer of myself.

She was a veteran of several long-running Broadway shows, including *Fiddler on the Roof,* which she appeared in with Bette Midler. She assured me that there were plenty of roles for mature gentlemen like myself and that I could be on Broadway one day! Since I was only sixty at the time, I had my whole life ahead of me.

We worked together for what must have been nearly five years. At one point she encouraged me to join her in a gym class that took place in a studio in Carnegie Hall. Once a week, we would exercise with other aging show business types. It was an "older" crowd, to say the least; one of the ladies was ninety-nine years old and came to the class, rain or shine, ice or snow, wearing four-inch high heels and mini-skirts. After about a year, Ann decided I was ready to perform in public. She introduced me to a cabaret group that performed at Don't Tell Mamas, a small space on West 46th Street where aspiring singers joined other hopefuls, putting on little shows that lasted an hour.

Ann told me when I performed that I should sing to the wall, that imaginary place somewhere above the heads of the audience. Never lock eyes with a spectator, she warned. On the night of my debut, the audience was rather sparse. I realized that most of the people—twenty-five or so—sitting at the tiny, wobbly tables in a rather moldy-smelling, dark room were relatives and friends of the performers who had been gang-pressed into attending. I had co-opted my partner and another friend from out of town who was visiting us to be there.

My number was a duet that I was to perform with a beautiful Irish American girl who actually did have a really good voice. We were going to sing "People Will Say We're in Love" from the musical *Oklahoma!* It was a song that required an assertive, confident male singer on the order of Howard Keel, who had played the part in the musical. Veronica was to enter from stage left, and I was supposed to join her coming from the opposite side. The pianist played the opening bars of the song, I saw lovely Veronica glide onto the stage and look longingly in my direction as I sat in a chair off-stage.

The pianist repeated the opening notes to the song, and I continued to sit in my chair. This occurred yet a third time, with Veronica alone on stage. Somehow I had forgotten that I was supposed to be in this number and be on stage myself! No shrinking violet, Veronica then took the situation in hand, marched over, jerked me off the chair, and dragged me on stage. Looking slightly bewildered, I put my arms around her and began my part in the duet as the macho cowboy. My embrace looked more like I was clinging to my mother for help. The audience roared with laughter. Not exactly the reaction we had anticipated for this romantic duet. And thus my show business career was launched.

Ann, of course, continued to be supportive and told me I had "nailed it" in my duet at Mamas. She encouraged me to participate in other group shows, which I did for several more years. Veronica, my unfortunate duet partner, had by now become a good friend. She encouraged me to keep on singing, but discretely suggested that I might want to join a chorus and sing as part of a group. I replied that I had no interest in choruses and wanted to sing solo! For an aspiring performer, there are no compromises! No such thing as being realistic.

Ann, who had never had a sick day in her life, died suddenly at eighty-three. Two days before she passed away, I visited her in her tiny flat. When I walked into the apartment, she was being transferred from her bed to the sofa in her living room, and because of her considerable weight, the attendant had rolled her onto a sheet and was dragging her across the floor. She peered up at me from this humiliating position and, with a bright smile, said, "Nice day! Come on in!"

After Ann's death, I took a break for a while and then I found another teacher. Through the singers' drum system and word of mouth, I ended up with Roscoe, who lived in Hell's Kitchen in a fifth-story walk-up. I called the place Heart Attack Hotel and arrived at his doorstep every week seriously winded. Roscoe was entertaining and lots of fun, but not much of a voice teacher.

Overweight, he was always dieting and followed a high-protein regimen that required the consumption of lots of meat, which he was always boiling in a large pot when I came for my lesson. His tiny flat reeked of the smell of boiled bones and discarded gristle. I found the stench of simmering beef and gamey lamb rather nauseating and spent most of my sessions with Roscoe on the verge of vomiting.

Roscoe did have some interesting stories to tell. He was good friends of the Mayflower Madame, the lady from the Philadelphia society family who had gone into the world's oldest profession as a procurer. It had been all over the papers, and he said they were planning a cabaret act. He told me about another friend named Rachel who had lots of problems and was unhappy in her marriage. She was super intelligent and very depressed and decided to take her life by throwing herself in front of a subway train.

Roscoe said Rachel had planned her death leap very carefully, standing on the platform for hours watching train arrivals and departures and timing and measuring just where the subway cars stopped. On the appointed day, very early in the morning, she went to the 7th Avenue line station and, dressed in black so as to be undetectable to the on-coming train, she lowered herself onto the track and waited. The train arrived and did its work; the only thing was Rachel had somehow miscalculated and in instead of killing herself, she had only managed to have her right arm and leg severed.

Fast forward two or three years. Rachel met somebody over the internet while she was recovering, and minus an arm and a leg now lives happily with that woman in Arizona. Roscoe wasn't sure if there was a moral to this tale. But between the severed body parts and the stench of rancid beef, I was out of there. I told Roscoe that I was moving to Japan and therefore had to curtail our lessons. In retrospect, that was a stupid thing to say. I should have just told him that I had run out of money, which was also true.

New York City is a really small place, and sooner or later you end up bumping into everybody you ever knew on the street. Of course, that happened with me and Roscoe one day. He glared at me, and I knew this was just one more nail in my coffin as a Broadway star.

Over the next couple of years, I went through a variety of voice teachers and coaches. One lady who lived in Chelsea had a photograph in her bathroom of Louis Jourdan, the star of *Gigi*, sitting on the toilet with the caption "Efforts" under the picture.

Another teacher had a hundred-pound Rottweiler named Blossom, who sat on my feet while I vocalized. I was the lucky one. Sometime later, Blossom went berserk and started attacking students whom she didn't quite like, taking large chunks from their legs. I was coming to an interesting conclusion about my multiple and various voice teachers and what I was learning.

My instrument, as they say in the trade, may not have been that good, and I was probably able to empty a room faster than a five-alarm fire bell, but I felt I had gotten a lot out of the experience. I had struggled through a series of shrinks earlier in my life, trying to deal with a variety of issues from guilt to depression to lack of confidence. That kind of therapy had no positive effect on me.

Quite the contrary. In fact, dealing with psychiatrists, who are a pretty depressing breed of animal themselves, made me even unhappier. But vocalizing in front of a voice teacher with a good piano accompanying me, I felt like a million dollars. Never mind that I sounded like yesterday's warmed-over omelet and that people hearing me sing had said "Don't quit your regular job!" When I was belting out a ballad, I felt all was right with the world, and my spirits soared!

So here I am, where I belong, back in the shower, happy singing to myself. It might be a tune from *South Pacific*. I seem to favor "Younger than Springtime" or perhaps if I'm in a somber mood, "Not While I'm Around" from that dark, wonderful murder-musical, *Sweeney Todd*. The only thing is, this time, I won't be warbling in the Y shower or any other public place. Just me at home alone. Well, maybe my two cats will pick up the melody and start howling along with me.

CHAPTER FIFTEEN

SIC TRANSIT THE GOOD OLD TIMES
An Abandoned Swimming Pool Brings Back Happy Memories

For nearly twenty years, on weekends and holidays, my refuge from the pressurized urban life was my friend George's farm. Located an hour and a half north of New York City, a stone's throw from the village of Montgomery, it was a haven of tranquility, especially during long, hot summers—the jewel in the crown being George's swimming pool.

George started farming back in the thirties when he was a youngster and plowing fields was no picnic. He used to talk about how his workday on the farm started before it was light, feeding the livestock then harnessing the team of horses he would struggle with for eight hours to ready hundreds of rows of black soil for planting. Before he was born, his grandmother had been dragged to her death by a spooked team of horses as she plowed those same fields in her long skirts.

Sometime in the sixties, George decided to build a pool—his only extravagance in an otherwise frugal farmer's life—and it was his pride and joy. Not quite Olympic-sized, it sat next to his nineteenth-century farmhouse, bordering on fields of cabbage and corn with a distant mountain view. It was sparkling clean, and its clear, blue water was always inviting. In the immaculate garden and grounds surrounding it, not a blade of grass was out of place. Riots of flowers decorated the pool patio from spring till autumn frost.

One year George kept the pool open well into October, and its heated water sent up clouds of mist, making us feel we had been transported to some exotic Icelandic spa. On those lazy summer days, we swam, read, relaxed around the pool and ate our meals on the patio—leisurely breakfasts, lunches, and dinners cooked with ingredients from the local roadside farmers' stands.

For special events like birthdays, George would organize more elaborate affairs with lanterns strung around. Sometimes at night torches were lit, their flames reflected in the pool's still water. In the country tradition still alive in his area, neighbors would bring freshly baked pies, cakes, and other local delicacies when they came for a swim. Once there was a Hawaiian-themed dinner party; it didn't matter that the only things Hawaiian were the rings of canned pineapple in the salad and Don Ho hula music. For nearly two decades, George's pool had been my favorite escape, better than any Mediterranean cruise or exotic tropical island.

Late in the afternoon one August, maybe a dozen years ago, George was busy preparing for a crowd of visitors to descend on the pool for dinner and had forgotten to buy candles and some other provisions. I was dispatched to the local super market a couple of miles away and told to hurry back so that everything would be in apple-pie order before the guests arrived. On the way to the store, taking off from a stop sign at a blind turn on the country road, I broad-sided a speeding teenager, tossing his car into midair before totaling it. Miraculously, we both emerged without a scratch. Within minutes of the collision, police were on the scene, and before long I was cleared to go, my half-crushed car limping back to the farm, my hands shaking so violently I could barely steer.

At the house, the party was in full swing. Nobody noticed I had been gone so long, and it was the best thing that could have happened. Before I could even utter a word, George hustled me out to the pool to tend bar and then put me to work grilling steaks. I was so busy I forgot about the near-death encounter that had occurred an hour earlier.

Several years ago, decades of back-breaking labor began to take their toll on George. As he described it, his body "just plum give out." George was incapacitated and began spending long periods of time in a nursing home. But recently he went home for a spell, and I drove up to the farm to visit him for a few hours. Sitting around the kitchen table, his border collie Molly at his feet, he and I reminisced about the good old times and talked about various friends and neighbors who had enjoyed his hospitality over the years.

Although wheelchair-bound and hard of hearing, George had lost none of his keen sense of humor or his joy of living. When it came time for me to go back to the city, he smiled as I shouted good-bye, still cutting a handsome figure in his farmer's flannel shirt. As I crossed the driveway to my car, I noticed the pool house, forlorn in the late afternoon light, its gray paint peeling. On impulse, I walked over and opened the sagging gate to the pool. What greeted me was a haunting reminder that nothing in life stays the same. George's pristine pool was unrecognizable. It hadn't been used since he became unwell, and its cover had ripped open, revealing swamplike green liquid underneath. A torn pool house awning flapped in the wind, and an empty tin can rolled on the once pristine patio, now a weed-infested wasteland. As I stood silently contemplating what it all meant, I heard the sound of laughter and splashing water. Later, driving back to the city, I was glad I had opened that pool gate and released so many happy memories.

Made in the USA
Middletown, DE
27 April 2016